CW01623598

How to Be a Comedian and Smash Your First Gig

LOUISE STEVENSON

ISBN: 978-1-8381307-0-1

Table of Contents

Acknowledgements

Quotes: by Sarah Millican, William Faulkner, Will Rogers, Family Guy and Mark Twain, Cynthia Hymel, and The Greatest Showman.

Comedian Advice: from Dara O'Briain, Reece Shearsmith, Tim Vine, Shappi Khorsandi, Sean Walsh, Eddie Izzard, Ed Byrne, Joe Lycett, Sean Loch, Harry Hill, and Milton Jones.

Case Study Contributors: Russell Heywood, Tony O'Hara, Polly Brown and Louise Wells.

Book References: *Tickling the English* Dara O'Briain

Joke Contributors: Dick David, Peter Kay, Jimmy Carr, Louise Stevenson, Stu Francis, Katherine Ryan, Danny Bhoy, Will March, Tim Vine, Wendy Liebman, and Michael Redmond.

Video Clips Recommendations: Peter Kay - *Biscuits.* Full show, *The Tour that Didn't Tour Tour*; Dara O'Briain - Watch *This is the Show* Stu Francis - One-Liners; Billy Connolly -*The National Anthem.*

Special Thanks: to Cover Designer Jessica Barrah and Readers/Editors Polly, Sarah, Paul M, Paul S and Ian.

.

Author Introduction

A very warm welcome to you. Thank you for picking this book.

My name is Louise Stevenson. I am a comedian, writer, and communications coach.

People often ask me, "What made you get into comedy?"

What MADE me?

It's like I'm under duress, with some sort of comedy pimp pushing me out onto the stage, night after night: "Make them laugh, bitch."

The truth is much more straightforward. I got into comedy because I loved making people laugh (and, with the help of my comedy pimp, I knew I could). The truth of it was, I thought I'm funny, I can do this. I know it's not something you can say out loud. It's like announcing "I'm gorgeous!" in public - not very British at all.

I'm a comedian with over twenty years' experience. I know the ins and outs of being a comedian, and I know the comedy industry. I have worked all over the world performing stand-up, and I still perform and compere regularly.

I started my comedy career in 1999 in Wellington, New Zealand. I worked the New Zealand and Australian circuit for several years before working the London circuit for five years. I enjoyed performing at the Edinburgh Fringe Festival after my first experience in a sell-out show *'Scotland's Best and Guests,'* many moons ago, which was a positive experience.

I was knocked out of Channel 4's *So You Think You're Funny* competition by Russell Brand. I had been the only female on the bill and put on first, like the sacrificial lamb. (No. I'm not bitter at all ha!) I've had the pleasure of working alongside some great comedians like Jimmy Carr, Sarah Millican, Alan Carr, Rich Hall, Frankie Boyle, and Lucy Porter, among many others.

A writer of fiction novels, I completed my first in a year, and after submitting my work, I secured a place on an MA Creative Writing course. I was awarded a Post Graduate Diploma and then a master's degree. I teach Creative Writing and Public Speaking, as well as Stand-up Comedy.

In this book, I draw from my twenty plus years of comedy experience and my ten plus years teaching comedy. I also use my writing expertise, which will help you create your comedy material and book your first gig.

The Beginning of the Comedy Courses.

I moved to Brighton, England, in 2003. In 2010, I was made redundant from a job I hated and decided to start my business teaching stand-up. And so, Brighton Comedy Course was born. Since then, thousands of people have come on the Beginners course, the Advanced, the Online courses, and the Comedy Weekenders. I started running comedy courses internationally too. If there's a demand, I'll be there.

Several graduates share management with big acts like Jo Brand and Dara O'Briain. Because of their talent and hard work, they've managed to obtain agents like Off the Kerb. Many come on the course to meet new friends, have fun, and grow in confidence. Some catch the comedy bug and discover they have a talent for it.

Throughout the book, there are case studies from Brighton Comedy Course graduates. They share their experiences of comedy courses, the comedy circuit and the challenges of stand-up. I hope you find inspiration in their stories.

Enhanced confidence is probably the most consistent feedback I receive in graduate reviews. Stand-up is a game-changer on that front. I knew when I was doing my first gig, I would never feel the same again.

People join courses for different reasons. For those with aspirations for fame, there's nothing wrong with wanting to be successful. However, you should know, despite the growing presence of comedians on television and in the media, there are easier ways to get on TV that mean way less work than as a stand-up comedian. Few TV and panel show comedians have spent less than eight to ten years working the circuit for little or no money, working their craft before finding the success they enjoy now.

Praise for *How to Be a Comedian and Smash Your First Gig.*

"If you want down to earth, no nonsense advice on starting and developing as a stand-up comedian then this book is for you. It is an easy read full of the author's advice and experiences which are always encouraging and realistic too.

The book is well structured taking you from the beginning to developing your set. There are a number of exercises along the way which you would be advised to immerse yourself in properly to get the most from the learning.

A book can't manifest the same human experience as being on a good stand up course but it's certainly the next best thing."
Simon Mills

"Even if you think you have no intention of getting up on stage then this book will make you want to and, even better, give you the tools to succeed. It's not just for aspiring comedians though. Anybody who wants to write will find nuggets of

inspiration and great ideas for generating material and kick starting their thought process. Whether you want to be live at the Apollo or give more polished presentations at work then this book is your friend."
Jo Terry

"Interested in taking your first steps into comedy? Then this is the book for you. Like a fitness regime for getting your jokes in shape, this outlines the steps needed to reach your goal. And, like any fitness regime, to reap the benefits you're going to have to do the work!

Think you're a great storyteller or more of a one-liner comedian? This book shows you how to deconstruct a comedy set so you'll know exactly how to build the strongest set of your own. It's filled with great practical advice, from where to find material for your jokes, to invaluable stage techniques to aid your delivery." Tony O'Hara

Here's what Brighton Comedy Course graduates said about the Comedy Courses:

"I LOVED doing the course. I talked about doing something like this for years and finally took the plunge. Louise is a Brilliant Tutor. It was EPIC!" Charlie Fitzgerald

"I completed Louise's eight-week comedy course and graduation gig, and I can honestly say it's one of the best things I've ever done. Not only have I learned tonnes, but I'm buzzing from my first ever stand-up. I've met some hilarious like-minded people, and I've had a two-month mood boost that would make a therapist envious. To anyone considering it, I say give it a try; you have nothing to lose." Sophie Fyles

"This course was everything I needed to get the knowledge and confidence to do stand-up comedy. Louise is a great teacher. She gets you performing straight away. (I) Highly recommend (her) to anyone who fancies themselves at stand-up comedy. The graduation gig at the end is fantastic. Pretty much guaranteed to get everyone laughing." Harvey Dann

"If you have ever considered getting up on stage and trying stand-up comedy, this is the course for you! This course will give you the confidence to turn ideas you think are funny into material that will make an audience laugh! I thoroughly recommend booking up!" Scott Gnilsog

"This course has been so much fun. It's a supportive environment to get confident and ready to perform … I wish I hadn't put it off for so long! If you're thinking about it, just do it!" Cath Bailey

I love comedy, and I'm looking forward to sharing my knowledge and experience with you.

LET'S GET STARTED.

Introduction

Welcome to How to Be a Comedian and Smash your first Gig. Great to have you on board.

You'll need Internet access, a notepad and pen, and a laptop, tablet, or computer to complete this course.

Guidelines for Completing this Book

This is a practical book. For the best shot at success, you should take the time to complete each writing exercise and do the homework.

The theory will give you a good idea of the job and how to do it, but the method on its own is useless. Practice makes perfect when it comes to writing jokes.

By completing the exercises, you'll start developing the writing discipline crucial for a comedian.

This book provides step by step instructions in helping you reach your first gig. Each chapter will take around an hour to complete. Try and complete each section in one sitting. Put regular time aside to work through the book in as short a time frame as possible. Doing so will help compact your learning and build momentum.

An achievable amount of time to complete this book is two weeks. It's a marathon, not a sprint. This duration will allow you to complete the exercises, pick up the theory and let it sink in consciously (and subconsciously). You'll soon switch into comedy mode and gain the confidence you need for your first gig. This book is not just about being a stand-up comedian. It's about being a GREAT stand-up comedian, a comedian who is professional and stands out from the crowd.

Accountability. Brighton Comedy Course students love the accountability of the courses. This book requires the same level of responsibility. There will be checkpoints throughout asking where you are on your journey. Expect questions such as:

Are you writing regularly?
Are you completing the homework?
Are you watching comedy?
Are you going to comedy gigs?

If you want to be a stand-up comedian, you'll need to put in the effort, complete the tasks and immerse yourself in the comedy world.

Here's what you should start doing right away:

Start watching more comedy.

It's best to watch live gigs if you can. If possible, mix it up. Go to the bigger, more established clubs as well as the open mic nights. They will inspire you and give you some idea of the 'type' of comedian you want to be. Most countries I've been to have had a few local comedy nights. Larger cities often have a thriving comedy scene, so you'll have plenty of choices. Do a quick Google search or look at a What's On guide in your chosen area.

TV and comedy DVDs work too. Start watching comedy with an analytical head. What do you like? What don't you like? What does the comedian use for laughs apart from words?
Do the comedians make use of accents, musical instruments, physical gestures, facial expressions, or singing? Comedians will use every trick in their arsenal to make a gig funny.

Start thinking about what makes you laugh and when you've made people laugh. It's good to identify what makes you tick. It will help when it comes to writing material.

Get a Notepad

The first thing I tell my students when they start the Beginners' Comedy course is to get their hands on a notepad. Sitting down to write stand-up can be tough. You can make it easier by writing down your ideas (or any funny situations) as they come to you. I suggest you always have your notebook on hand; so when you start writing, you'll have a smorgasbord of comedy ideas from which to draw.

You may think, "I'll remember that." There's a good chance you won't.

I remember when, one night, I had to get up four or five times to write down comedy ideas. It was annoying, but it turned into a funny little set.

Recording your thoughts on your phone can work too. I prefer getting things down on paper, but you must do what works for you. You can choose to open a new file on your PC for comedy writing if you like.

As Sarah Millican once said, "A notepad is your friend. Your memory is not."

Find a Routine Time to Write

Put aside a regular time to write. For example, it could be on a Saturday morning from 10:00 to 12:00 or a Wednesday evening from 6:00 to 9:00.

Writing is crucial for a comedian. You should write as much as possible. The more you write, the better chance you have of producing successful material. I recommend spending at least three to five hours a week with the exercises in this book. Hopefully you'll find the time to do more.

Write wherever you can - on tedious train journeys, at work (preferably during lunchtime or, if you can skive, during work. But if you work for me, that's a no!)

Split your dedicated comedy time into three sections. E.g. if I spend six hours a week on my comedy, I'll:

Write for two hours
Edit for two hours
Rehearse it out loud for two hours

Should You Book Your First Gig?

I recommend waiting until you've completed this book. There's no desperate hurry. You want your first gig to be the best it can be.

It will take a fair amount of writing, editing, and learning the craft of stand-up, so best wait.

When you go and watch live comedy, you can take the opportunity to say hello to the promoter and the comedians.

Tell them you enjoyed the show. This is a great way to lay the groundwork. Then you can hit them up for a gig when you're ready.

My Humble Beginnings

I can't remember a definitive moment when I decided to become a comedian. I always enjoyed watching comedians on the TV when I was a child. Billy Connolly was my first experience with stand-up comedy. He was a trailblazer and is now a comedy legend.

In 1969, my mum gave birth to the first boy into an almost all-girl family. I was born three years later. I know it's not China, where boys are highly coveted, but there were definite similarities. I was in my brother's shadow and didn't enjoy it at all. There's nothing more tragic than a show-off without an audience.

Humour was (and still is) a valued commodity in Glasgow and very much so in my home. I used to look for any way to make my family laugh. I experimented with some dodgy impressions of famous TV characters, all of which reveal my old age. Some of you won't remember Frank Spencer and Rigsby from Rising Damp. I'm sure, though, even the youngest among you will be familiar with my specialty, Miss Piggy!

I wouldn't say stand-up was a burning ambition for me when I was growing up. There were few women comedians. That may have had an impact, though I loved making people laugh (I still do!)

While backpacking around Australia at the age of twenty-seven, the appeal of making people laugh on a bigger platform grew stronger. I confided in a few close friends, and though they ribbed me mercilessly, they were incredibly supportive.

I met street performer buddies who suggested learning tricks (and I don't mean the sexual kind) for street performance. They thought if I could master street performance, I could do anything.

So, naturally, I joined the circus.

Yep. It was a postcard that elicited much despair on its arrival in Glasgow: "Guess what she's done now!"

I started my circus career as a candy floss girl and ended up as a lighting and music technician. I always used to mix up the animals' music. Confused tigers would enter the ring to the dog's *Mission Impossible* soundtrack. Ever been given the deadeye by a tiger? Scary!

After three months, I left the circus with one circus skill: I could juggle three balls. Not totally convinced I had enough for a street show, I headed for Wellington, New Zealand. I got a job in a bar, and that's where the story starts. One night I met an English comedienne and confessed I wanted to perform stand-up. She smiled and told me she ran comedy courses. Even better, she had space on one starting the next day! Maybe some things are meant to be.

So, I started a Beginners comedy course. I loved it, and the environment was supportive. I adored the camaraderie between the aspiring comedians. Support and friendship are two massive benefits of doing a comedy course.

I wrote lots of comedy and performed each week in class. On the run-up to my first gig, I was so nervous, but I remember thinking, "I can do this." I went over my material at every possible opportunity. I'd rehearse as I set up the bar for the day. I'd rehearse again on my way home. When I arrived at home, I'd rehearse in front of the mirror with a hairbrush as my mic.

The day finally came, and I felt nervous but ready. I performed in a little room called the Blue Note to twenty Kiwi Goths. They'd had little exposure to a Glaswegian accent though, and strangely, lots of exposure to the Proclaimers.

There seems to be at least one Proclaimers song in every jukebox in New Zealand (and Oz). Lucky for me, I had a Proclaimers joke as the crescendo of my gig! It may have been that joke which got me my first booking, or maybe the audience wanted a language challenge.

I was delighted I'd done okay, though I'd be lying if I didn't admit I felt a slight deflation. There had been a massive build-up, and I didn't have any close friends or family in the country to come and watch my first gig. That said, I was 100% sure I wanted to do it again.

Hopefully, you will too.

It's Your Turn. Take Between Thirty to Sixty Minutes to Complete this Exercise. Good Luck.

I would like you to list the reasons why you want to do stand-up.

What is it about comedy that gets your blood pumping? What is it about YOU that makes you want to do stand-up? Be as honest as possible with yourself.

There are no right or wrong answers to these questions. However, as I said before, if your dream is to become rich and famous, there are easier ways to do it.

If your dream is to get laid, then aim higher (though male comedians seem to do quite well).

Congratulations! You've finished the first chapter! Now, let's crack on.

What You Need to Know about Stand-up

- There are no hard and fast rules for becoming a successful comedian.
- There are many different styles of comedy. What works for one comedian may not work for another. Imagine Jack Dee doing upbeat, slap-stick comedy or Jo Brand playing a ditzy airhead. You should experiment with different genres and styles of comedy to see what works best for you.
- NOTE - I can't make you funny (Sorry, no refunds). What I CAN do is give you advice and a range of methods to help you tap into your comedy genius.
- The aim of this book is to help you grow in confidence. By the end of the book (or even before) you should be comfortable generating ideas and writing them down. It's all about finding the balls to produce material and put it out there.

It's Your Turn. Take Approximately Thirty Minutes to Complete This Exercise. Good Luck.

Write about the last time you genuinely belly laughed. It could have been at work, something you saw on the TV, or a conversation you overheard on the bus. What about it made you laugh?

Check-In: How was that? Could you think of a time?
Was it the sarcasm, stupidity, or absurdity of the situation that made you laugh? Start taking notice of what makes you chuckle.

If you can tap into your sense of humour and know what makes you tick, it will help when you start writing material.

There are tonnes of opinions on how long it takes to become a successful comedian.

However, most comedians agree on the "Eight to ten years" mark.

Some think it takes around 10,000 hours of application before a person is good at any one thing. Others go as far as to say, "It isn't worth listening to a comedian until they've been on the circuit for a decade."

I don't agree. Experience and hard work are necessary, yes; but comics have become exceptionally successful in a much shorter timeframe.

And, of course, someone could put in 10,000 hours of practice and STILL be rubbish. It takes time to master the skill of stand-up, but it takes talents (and some luck!) too.

I've known comedians who've got into their groove and found management within two years. Kevin Bridges was booked for paid gigs within four months of starting stand-up. This is unusual but not impossible.

Remember these words from Sarah Millican: "Being funny is not enough. You have to work hard."

Fame

Many fantastic comedians on the circuit have chosen to avoid the limelight and instead, work on their craft. Many of these comedians elicit a tremendous amount of respect from their peers.

There's nothing wrong with wanting to be famous. That said, the comedians filling big stadiums, like Jimmy Carr, Amy

Schumer, or Peter Kay, all spent YEARS working stages around the country and paying their dues.

The Ups and Downs of Being a Stand-Up Comedian

Stand-up comedy is a tough industry. If you want to make comedy a career, you need to know the harsh truth: Most comedians work a long time to find any level of fame - if they ever do.

While there are more opportunities for comics to appear on TV, many comedians don't make it to the small screen.

If you want to make it and become a top comedian, perseverance is vital.

The following are a few pros and cons to consider before embarking on a comedy career. The list isn't to put you off. It's to arm you with the facts.

If you still want to go ahead after knowing the pros and cons, you are in a stronger position. Remember to take everything one step at a time, craft your material, do your first gig, and continually work the local stages.

The Downs

- It can pay little or nothing for years.
- It can be challenging to juggle comedy with a 9-5 job, especially if you want to travel for gigs.
- Traveling to gigs can be expensive. At the beginning of your journey, you'll be lucky to simply cover the costs.
- Audience size can vary. One night an audience could be thirty or more; the next it could be a handful, which is

not unusual. I'll always remember one Sunday night in London when my housemates ordered pizza and opened a bottle of wine. I had to leave for a gig on the other side of London for no payment. I ended up performing to an audience of four. It takes real discipline, especially for unpaid gigs, to leave the house.

What I can say is these gigs are perfect dress rehearsals for the Fringe festivals. With so much choice at the Fringe, four could be the size of your average audience.

- There is a LOT of travel involved in stand-up, especially if you want as much stage time as possible. I've had many long car journeys, sometimes stuck in a traffic jam for hours. A six-hour car journey for a ten-minute gig is much more typical than you'd think.

- Writing good material can take hours. (Actually, so can bad material.) Writing is a considerable time investment.

The Ups

- The buzz you get from making people laugh is bloody fantastic! It's a high unmatched by anything else. (Yes, even that!)

- There's also the instant gratification. A writer can be planning, writing, and producing a book for years before he or she knows if an audience will like it. With stand-up, you'll know instantly.

- The monetary gain can be great if you make a name for yourself. There are plenty of people who make a good living from comedy.

- The keyword here is "successful". For these comedians,

there's the opportunity to work two well-paid gigs in one night (often in the bigger cities). Fees in clubs vary, but some comedians make the UK's average weekly salary over one weekend.

- Of course, if established, a comedian could make a few more bucks through TV, books, and movies.

- The adulation and applause are a massive plus also. Hearing someone say how much they laughed or how much you cheered them up never gets old.

- You meet loads of hilarious and exciting people.

So, What Do You Need to be a Comedian? You Need:

- To be funny

- Determination and courage to bounce back

- Motivation and enthusiasm

- Discipline to write and practice

- Patience

Other Helpful Things to Have:

- A car or access to lifts

- Excellent communication skills - If you want regular work, you need to get on with promoters and comedians. (They can often be the same person.)

- Savvy sales skills - You'll need these when booking gigs, especially when you start getting paid.

- Access to a big city or town where you can get regular stage time. You may want to move to a bigger city, depending on your motivation to succeed.

It's Your Turn! Take Between Thirty and Sixty Minutes to Complete This Exercise. Good Luck.

This Exercise is in Three Parts.

Part 1: Off the top of your head, write down some subjects you might want to make into a routine. Don't overthink it; just write. Make a list.

Part 2: Now look at your list. Does any item stand out?

Below this paragraph is a spider chart. Spider charts are a great way of generating ideas around a central topic. The beauty of spider charts is they remove the inner critique saying, 'Is that funny enough?". It doesn't need to be funny just yet. Right now, you're simply generating ideas. Spider charts remove any pressure.

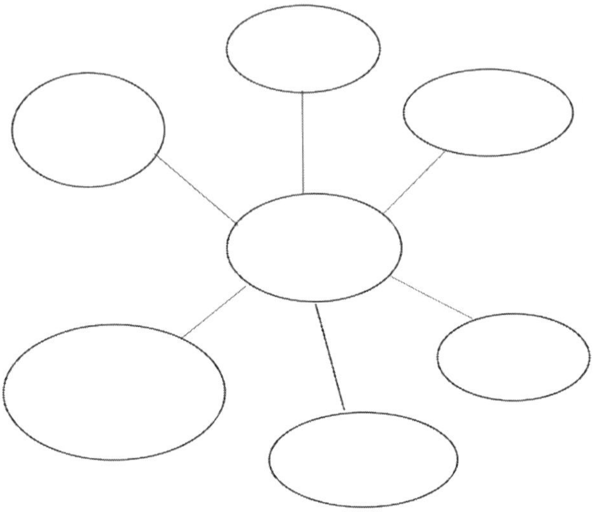

Draw a spider chart in your notebook. Look at your list and choose the topic that stands out. Put that topic in the middle bubble of the map.

For example, if I had the subject "celebrity" in the middle of my map, my chart may look like this.

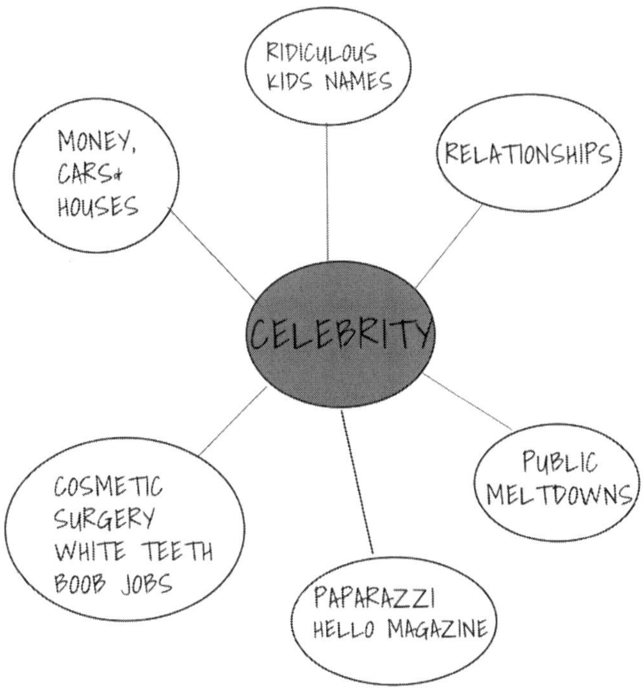

Part 3 - Take ten minutes to complete your spider chart with your chosen topic. Fill in as many bubbles as possible. Add more bubbles if needed. If your subject takes you in a different direction, that's fine. Flesh out as many ideas as possible.

Check-in: How did you get on? How did you find completing the exercise? Easily? With difficulty? Do you now have a page bursting with ideas?

Well done. Use spider charts regularly to write material. I find spider charts an excellent way to kick-start writing sessions. They help me get the creative juices flowing.

If you struggled to come up with ideas, try choosing another topic from your list.

The best way to use spider charts is to write whatever comes to mind. Spider charts will provide the ideas for your material when you're ready to write. It doesn't need to be perfect right away!

Hold on to your spider charts. You'll need them again.

How to Write Material

So, we've used our spider chart to flesh out our ideas. The most important thing is to ignore your inner critic.

Don't overthink it! Just write whatever comes to mind, and remember:

- The first draft is just to get your ideas down. It doesn't have to be super funny at this point. That's why we have the editing process.

- Let your hair down regarding whatever topic you've chosen. Write down any train of thought that comes to mind. You may wind up going down another path, and that's fine too. Don't stop writing. Go with the flow.

- Ask yourself, "Why is this particular topic on my mind? What does it make me feel? Does anybody else notice it? What can be done about it?"

  Let's go back to the "celebrity" example. Imagine if you called your child 'FiFi Trixie-Belle'. Imagine the response from your family and friends. How would the child get on at your local school? What about when they're older and trying to find work?

- Let your mind run with the possibilities of how their name could affect their lives.

- After you've jotted down your ideas, see if anything stands out. Is there anything you want to focus on and expand?

- You may find a golden nugget from three pages of written A4. Sure, it won't be scream-worthy award-winning material yet, but it's a seed that could sprout into something special

- Your chosen topic may grow as you get out and about and allow inspiration to come to you.

It's Your Turn! Take Between Thirty and Sixty Minutes to Complete this Exercise. Good Luck.

Look at your spider chart from the last chapter. Read over the ideas you wrote in the bubbles.

Have a go at writing some material! It's only a first draft, so relax and have fun with it.

Check-in: How did you get on? Did you find it to be easy or difficult? More importantly, did you enjoy it?

Writing good material is an art form. It can be hard at first. However, if you learn to quash your inner critic and just write, you'll be surprised how quickly your writing improves.

The More You Write, the Better You Become.

Tips on Writing:

- Keep everything you write, store it away, and check it out later. It may take shape later or fit nicely with other material.

- Write every day. You don't necessarily have to write jokes; but writing is a skill, and within a few weeks or months, you will see the quality of your writing improve.

- Try writing ten jokes a day. You might end up with one or two that make it on stage; but if you produce one working joke a week, you'll end up with fifty-two new jokes a year.

- Don't be afraid to write crap. Everybody does. Remember - it's a numbers game.

- Material must be written, performed, edited, performed again, restructured or reworded, and honed to be its best. Sometimes it's more about the performance of the material than the writing itself. Maybe the punchline needs to be elsewhere, or it can be enhanced with an action or facial expression or timed with a pause before it's delivered.

- Allow yourself to pursue tangents. If something takes you, go with it.

- Try to connect with your material. How does each joke fit with the next and the overall set?

- Try writing each joke on a card. Writing this way is a good way of trying out new material and keeps each joke separate. The cards are good for rehearsing material; but try to avoid taking notes and cards on the stage. If you feel you must, do so only on open mic nights and not for paid clubs. The cards are handy for the review process. When you've finished a gig, separate the cards into piles - one pile for jokes that worked and one pile for jokes that didn't work. If it helps, pin the cards on a pin board and rearrange the structure of your gig to find out where the material best fits.

To reiterate, your best chances of producing good material are to:

1. Write, write, write! The more you write, the better chance you'll have of producing successful material.

2. Ignore your inner critic.

3. Find regular times to write - when you know you won't be interrupted.

4. Commit to a good amount of writing time per week. Three to five hours is a good starting point.

5. Don't look for other things to do, e.g. clean the underside of the tap, arrange your books in alphabetical order, etc. Keep your focus on writing.

6. Find your own voice and style. Experiment.

7. Be yourself. Your material will be funnier, and your delivery will be more natural (unless of course you are performing as a comedy character).

8. I love intelligent comedy. It's not for everyone. Be intelligent if it's who you are, but keep in mind you don't need to be too clever. A lot of great topics are common, ordinary, or mundane.

It's Your Turn! Take between Thirty and Sixty Minutes to complete this exercise. Good Luck.

This exercise is broken up into two parts:

1. Watch at least half an hour of a stand-up performance - on TV, DVD, online, or a live gig.
   Write the name of the comedian in your notepad. What subjects did he or she use for material?

   Did you think the performance worked for the comedian? If so, why do you think it did or didn't?

2. Choose another subject from your material topic list or another topic of your choice. Flesh out the idea by spider chart and write material based on the topic. I would suggest spending a minimum of one hour to complete this task. Good Luck!

Tips on Writing from the Best

In this chapter, I've compiled advice from established comedians working the comedy circuit. A few of them discuss inventing their material on stage.

Improv is a brave move during a performance, and I certainly encourage it.

I'm a big fan of preparation - writing, editing, and rehearsing material before going on stage, especially when starting out as a comedian.

It's worth noting the different approaches and what may or may not work for you.

Tim Vine is a one-liner comedian. We'll discuss one-liner comedians in more detail later.

Tim writes fifteen new jokes a day on a postcard, and he often works backward. He starts with the punchline, then works towards the setup.

He says: "I hear punchlines every day in conversation, and I think how we can get there in a different way. For example, if someone says, 'Serves him right,' I think, 'Okay... a friend of mine's got his left arm missing. Serves him right.'"

Shappi Khorsandi is an Iranian-born British comedian, who started stand-up in 1997.

"In stand-up, the most important stuff goes on before any of the actual writing happens. I'll have a strong emotional response to something, an incident, something I've seen or heard. If it dances about my head bothering me, I get on stage and say it in front of an audience."

"If I'm relaxed enough, a punchline will eventually arrive. Then I write it down, do it better, and write that down. Each time I write it down, it becomes sharper."

Sean Walsh: "I don't really write my stuff. I don't type it. It's bad, I know that. I just sort of have an idea and then I go up there (on stage) and do it. And then it sticks, and that's the way it is."

"I keep meaning to Tweet a picture of my Edinburgh show--it's one piece of paper, some arrows, and about *twenty* words on it just scribbled together. That's the Edinburgh show."

Eddie Izzard is a legend. I think we all agree on that! Here's what he has to say about the writing process.

"In stand-up, it helps to play yourself and talk about your own feelings. You cannot fail to be original if you're just talking about what you think of X, Y or Z."

I think, when you watch Eddie Izzard, you can almost see the cogs moving, and you're aware he's making up stuff as he goes along. He comes up with material on stage and hones it in the live environment.

"Sometimes, I write notes on what I want to talk about and start trying to flesh them out with the to-ing and fro-ing of chit-chat; but it's still tricky. It's so much easier to find that on stage. Most of it is adlibbed at some point."

Ed Byrne: "One thing that's changed in my writing is that I don't have to pretend to think of something for the sake of a joke. I mean, there's always comic exaggeration and embroidering a story to make it funnier, but it's truer to my life now.

I used to say I hated kids, for example. It wasn't true. I've always loved kids, but that wouldn't have fit with the kind of comic I was earlier in my career.

I think being truthful makes it *chancier*, but I take an opinion and try to find a way to make it funny - even if people don't agree with me. I think it pays off because audiences know what's authentic."

Joe Lycett: "My style is quite conversational, so the best stuff comes out from me having that conversation - actually talking out loud."

"But, that said, a lot of the stuff is written on stage, because you go into this weird zone where the piece has to get a laugh. It really forces something out of you from somewhere. So, it's a mixture of all things.

I'll make my observation when I'm out and about. I'll jot it down on my phone, and then I'll go through those observations and think what scenario might fit this.

I draw spider diagrams. That becomes a routine possibly, or it doesn't. Those that do have potential I try at new material nights."

Sean Lock: "I've always worked at it. I've always had an office, somewhere to go every day to sit down and write. You may produce nothing that day, but I know it doesn't come easy. There's no easy trick to it; you just graft, really.

I remember Frank Skinner saying to me years ago, 'If someone can do eight hours a day in a factory, I can do five or six hours sitting at a desk trying to write jokes, and that's what I've done over the years.'

My approach to it has always been that I want to do material that I find funny. I don't have any objectives with comedy. I don't have a message; I just try to make people laugh as I can in the time that I'm up there."

Harry Hill: "A lot of the time, it's just sitting down and thinking of ideas. That's the boring answer. Very rarely do you walk past something in the street and ideas pop into your head. It's just imagination. It's just the way you're wired really. The more you do it, the weirder you become in that sense.

Stand-up is so immediate. You can have an idea in the morning and get a laugh for it in the evening. No one else can tell you what to do, apart from the audience. The audience is the ultimate arbiter."

Harry Hill is famed for his work ethic. Perhaps it has something to do with his previous life as a doctor.

Milton Jones deals in one-liners, which are sharp, surreal, and often silly. He won the Perrier Best Newcomer award in 1996 and has appeared on TV, radio, and panel shows ever since.

"It's about turning things upside down - looking at things people say and thinking, 'What's the opposite of that?'"

He goes on to say every word has its role to play. One word can make all the difference.

Dara O'Briain: "I'm not sure how other comedians write jokes, but this is what works for me ... I sit in a room at night, chained to a desk with a bottle of wine. I have scraps of paper in front of me covered in scribbles. I'm banging anything down that vaguely resembles a joke or the opportunity for a joke or a joke's first cousin.

I stare at these and think how desperately unfunny they all are. Two glasses of wine in, I am now buzzing enough to forget myself and how self-conscious and contrived this whole process is. I talk to myself, and the ideas flesh out into little rants and associations.

This is where the funny starts to happen. It happens when I'm not thinking about it and just making up silly stuff and chatting away to myself as I bang a few funny things together. This will lead to a couple of half-jokes... maybe more.

After the fourth glass, I'm too drunk. I just sit there, happily remembering how funny I used to be, about two glasses ago!"

In summary: Comedians have different techniques for developing material. What they have in common is hard work.

From these insights, hopefully you get the sense writing is a large part of a comedian's daily routine. This means it needs to be for you too.

It's Your Turn! Take Between Thirty Minutes and an Hour to Complete this Exercise. Good Luck.

If you were to choose three pieces of advice from this chapter that resonate with you, what would they be?

Write them down on your notepad. Then write three action points from your observations.

Comedy Journey Case Study

Tony had been working a nine-to-five office job when he started the Beginners comedy course. He'd never been in front of an audience before, though he'd been considering it for a long time.

"People had said to me I should be a comedian, but seeing a friend do her graduation gig was the clincher. The training was invaluable. Without it, I never would have had the guts to write."

Tony enjoyed the comedy theory of the course. Specifically, he liked studying other comedians' performances, their structure, and different styles of jokes. Studying theory helped him think about what style of comedian he wanted to be.

"The practical side of the course is a great way to test jokes and hone the delivery. It made me appreciate why even professional comedians do warm-up shows. Until you try the joke out in front of an audience, you won't know if it works or not."

He added, "I gained a lot of self-belief, a whole new set of friends, and a real sense of achievement on the comedy course.

There was also a perfect mix of criticism, praise, and practical advice. The feedback each week was a crucial part of learning the skills."

Tony had been surprisingly calm before the gig.

"The graduation gig was fantastic. I was looking forward to it, and I had only a few nerves, but I think that was because I really put the work into preparing my set. I knew the routine back to front. The adrenaline rush after the gig is hard to describe. Making the audience laugh was a real rush. I also felt a great sense of togetherness with the other comedians."

The Graduation Night

He adds, "Aside from using the skills for stand-up, the training has helped me when I give presentations at work, standing in front of a crowd is no longer daunting. My confidence levels have risen. It's no coincidence I changed jobs since finishing the course and have way more self-belief now."

Tony has kept performing a steady stream of stand-up gigs since graduating from Brighton Comedy Course. He completed the advanced course, and, while honing his style, he has written a great deal of new material. I asked him if there had been anything about stand-up comedy which surprised him.

"It was great to discover the supportive network of other comedians. I thought it would be more dog eat dog, but the helpfulness and genuine support makes you feel like you're a part of a community. Overall, it's been great. It's so much fun making people laugh, discovering local venues and meeting other comedians."

I asked Tony if he had any advice for new comedians working the comedy circuit.

"Some nights can be hard work! Travelling to gigs where you don't get paid can be demoralizing, but to be successful you need to put in the groundwork. The hardest part is bouncing back from a bad gig. That's when you need a supportive group of other comedians who've been there too."

On stage, Tony shares the culture shock as an Irish man moving to Brighton, where he witnessed a man being arrested for shoplifting:

"Bay leaves. The thief loudly defended his actions, stating, "They were an essential ingredient!"

Tony has gone full steam ahead since graduating. He's had competition success in the South Coast Comedian of the Year and organised and compered a regular comedy night in a remote country pub, all of which had been a real thrill for him. Also, he performed at Sussex University, where he learnt a lot about playing to an audience who have English as their second language.

I see good things ahead for this Irish man. Keep an eye out for him.

Different Genres of Comedy

At this point, you're probably watching a lot of stand-up comedy.

Are you aware of the different styles of comedy?

Do you have a favourite?

We're going to look at a few of the most popular styles of comedy in more detail. We'll be looking at:

- Observational
- Storytelling
- One-liners
- Improvisational

Other Comedy Genres

There's a wide range of comedy out there. Here are a few examples:

- Character comedy: i.e., Paul and Pauline Calf, Ali G, Borat, Steve Coogan's Alan Partridge, Catherine Tate's nan, Lauren Cooper, *Little Britain*'s Marjorie Dawes, Bubbles Devere, and Vicky Pollard.
- Physical comedy: a whole routine about your physical appearance. Jo Brand does a lot of this
- Sketches.
- Comedian personas: Jack Dee is grumpy; Al Murray is a pub landlord; Lee Evans is manic ... and so on.

- Impression comedy: Bobby Davro and Rory Bremner.
- Ventriloquists: Nina Conti.
- Music-based comedians: Bill Bailey and Tim Minchin.
- Mockumentaries: *The Office.*
- Doc Brown: a comedian who uses rap.

Note: Comedy is all about experimenting. Find out what suits you and what style you enjoy writing.

Check-in: Take the opportunity to do a quick progress check. How are you doing?

Take half an hour to think about and answer the following questions:

1. Are you still using your notebook to write down ideas as they come to you?
2. Are you finding the notebook invaluable?
3. Are you watching lots of comedy, both live and online?
4. Is what you're learning helping to shape your first set?
5. Are you stockpiling material?
6. Are you feeling more confident about your comedy journey?

TAKE ACTION: You may discover you have things to do after answering these questions. Please take a minute to write down any action points that will help your comedy progress.

Observational Comedy

Observational comedy takes your observations of everyday things and makes them funny.

Things often get a laugh because they're true. For example: "A London tube station shut down as the escalators weren't working. Surely escalators without electricity are just stairs?" Danny Bhoy

Observational comedy is purely your perspective with a twist.

In the next four chapters, we are going to cover the most popular styles of comedy and watch clips of the best of these comedians in action.

You will need internet access. You will find examples readily available online. I'd also suggest watching a full show of any of these comedians as they are excellent examples of these genres of comedy.

When watching, I'd like you to take note of what other techniques and additional elements the comedians use for laughs. It could be anything from pulling faces and funny walks to actions and accents. Observational comedy is one of the most popular styles of stand-up in the world, especially in the UK.

Google: Peter Kay, *Biscuits* - Watch this Clip Before Moving On.

Check-in: What did you think? Funny? It's interesting to think that a routine about biscuits would be so successful.

Peter Kay could have had a spider chart with "Biscuits" written in the middle. There is material in everything. This clip makes the point beautifully.

Pros

- There are millions of subjects from which to choose of which an audience will identify.

- It's easy to make related gags.

- This style is already hugely popular

- Observational comedy lends itself to a conversational style, so it comes off as natural.

Cons

- Making something relatable to everybody is difficult. Perspectives change from person to person. Your job, religion, upbringing, nationality, or class could all provide different views.

  You must find a common perspective within your audience or provide enough context for them to understand yours.

- It can be repetitive: "I saw... I think... I heard."

- There's a danger of it being too mundane.

I've seen some mundane subjects work brilliantly on stage. While doing a gig in Australia, I heard a comedian deliver a set about a computer keyboard. He went through most of the icons, and I found it hilarious.

He spoke about the "@" sign being redundant until email came along, then suddenly the @ turned into 'Mr. Popular.'

I've also heard fantastic sets about kitchen appliances. The premise of the joke being, when one breaks down, they all do ... like a conspiracy.

Tips

- Make sure the audience can relate to it.

- Write down your idea right away. Be as specific as possible, as this will help you remember the nuances which make the observation funny.

"First rule of comedy - be specific. You never say biscuit, you say Garibaldi." Reece Shearsmith

Observational Comedians

Kevin Bridges

Angela Barnes

Rhod Gilbert

Michael McIntire

Holly Walsh

Micky Flanagan

Jo Brand

James Ancaster

Gina Yashere

Q. Do You Think This is Your Style?

It's Your Turn! Take Between Thirty and Sixty Minutes to Complete this Exercise. Good Luck.

1. Choose a comedian from the list above and watch a clip of a show or the full show.

2. Write comedy material. Use a spider chart if it helps to flesh out the ideas. Choose a few subjects to produce three pages of observational comedy. It could be about family, work, terrible TV, food ... Don't overthink it. Just choose a subject and get down as many ideas from your perspective as you can.

3. When you run out of steam, choose another topic.

Check-in: How did you get on? Did you find it difficult? Or did you write loads?

Did you stifle your inner critic during the process?

Remember, writing will become easier the more you do it. Strengthen the writing muscle, and it will get stronger.

Storytelling

Growing up, storytelling comedians were among the first I watched. It had been a popular style that many TV comedians used in the 70s and 80s.

Storytelling is a set of anecdotes based (mostly) on your personal experiences.

We tell stories every day, and most of the media we consume is based on stories from other people's lives.

Researchers have found our brains are more active when we listen to stories. Storytelling is the oldest style of comedy, and it still thrives across most comedy circuits the world over.

Google: Billy Connolly, *The National Anthem* - Watch this Clip Before Moving On.

You will have noticed this is an old clip filmed in the 80s. You can tell by the celebrity audience, the fashion, and the hairstyles.

Some comedians excel at this style of comedy. I've chosen this clip for three reasons:

1. Billy Connolly is the master of storytelling, a trailblazer, and the leading innovator of this genre.

2. This is storytelling at its best.

3. It's a great example of owing the stage.

I went through the footage and noted down every second someone laughed. Here's what I found:

Billy Connolly National Anthem Laughter Hits

Seconds
10
30
37
40
44
48
53
57
05
11
16
22
25
36
41
47

I think you get the point. The average laugh gap is every eight seconds. One of the pitfalls of storytelling is thinking you can talk for four or five minutes, saving the laughs for the final punchline.

I think Billy's set makes the following point perfectly clear: Your punchline at the end should pack a punch with plenty of payoff for the audience. That said, the story needs to be punchy throughout.

Pros

- Storytelling allows you linger on one topic.
- It's a great way to connect with your audience.

- Storytelling allows more of your personality to shine.
- It enables the audience to see some of themselves in you - the shared experience.
- People's brains are hardwired to tune in to stories.

Cons

- Storytelling is not always ideal for a five-minute set, unless you've got punchlines littered throughout.
- If you choose to just have one punchline at the end, then the audience needs to believe the punchline will deliver a real payoff. They're investing their time in this story. A clap at the end doesn't necessarily mean the story had been a success. If the audience is quiet for most of the story, then it needs work.
- You need excellent editing skills to strip the story of surplus lines that don't add anything.
- The audience can tune out. Audience anticipation needs to be proportional to the time spent listening.

Tips and Things to Remember

- The difference between observational and storytelling is that storytelling has a beginning, middle, and end. Observational comedy can have those elements, but it doesn't need to.
- Storytelling works best when it's heartfelt.
- Avoid going into irrelevant detail. Forget the day or the street. Bring the funny.

- Make a connection with the audience before going into a story.

- Don't let the audience get in front of you. Have a few twists.

- Billy Connolly is a master storyteller, and he throws in physical comedy (making faces, silly walks, jumping up and down). This breaks up the story and adds to the hilarity.

Do You Think Storytelling is Your Style of Comedy?

Other Storytellers

Dave Allen

Aisling Bea

Daniel Kitson

Sarah Millican

Dylan Moran

Sarah Silverman

Eddie Izzard

Amy Schumer

Kevin Hart

It's Your Turn! Take Between Thirty and Sixty Minutes to Complete this Exercise. Good Luck.

1. Choose a comedian from the above list and watch a clip or a full show.
2. Have a go at writing storytelling comedy. Use a spider chart if it helps to flesh out ideas. Aim for three pages

of A4, if possible.

Check-in: How did you find it? I hope you're enjoying the writing. It should be challenging but fun. We're tapping into our funny bones and flexing our comedy muscles. Keep at it!

One-Liner Stand Up

One-liner comedy is a series of short jokes comprised of one or two sentences.

For example:

"I was raised as an only child ... which really annoyed my sister." Will Marsh

"Crime in multi-storey car parks ... That is wrong on so many levels." Tim Vine

Essentially, you need to go from the set-up to the punchline in the shortest timeframe possible.

These jokes can stand alone, and you can cover a range of subjects in one set. You can go from a joke about holidays to buying bread. (Comedy gold right there.)

It's best to give your set structure if you have a running theme threading jokes together.

Stewart Francis does this brilliantly in a set with an ongoing swimming gag.

There's not a huge number of comedians using this comedy style, so it's a niche in the market.

Performing in this style could allow you to stand out from the crowd on the glutted comedy circuit.

Google: Stewart Francis, *One-liners* **(**Watch this Clip Before Moving On.**)**

Pros

- You can cover a lot of topics.
- You'll keep the audience's attention as they'll need to concentrate.
- If a joke doesn't work, you can move straight on to the next one.
- It takes less time to produce a one-liner than a story.

Cons

- It takes a long time to build a set made up of successful one-liners.
- It can be difficult for an audience to get to know you.
- Prepare for a few groans! One-liners are often silly or slapstick. One or two moans is funny as it connects the audience; but if you use too many, you may lose your audience's faith in your ability.

Tips

One-liner comedy depends on having a twist. E.g. "The hardest thing about my grandmother's death (pause) was making it look like an accident." Dick David

You need to set the audience in one direction, then take them somewhere unexpected.

Here's another example from Stewart Francis: "We called our child after my wife's mother ... Passive-Aggressive Psycho turns five on Tuesday."

Remember, **here** are Two Simple Rules to One-Liner Comedy: There should be the shortest distance possible between the set-up and the punchline.

1. The set-up is short.
2. The punchline is always at the end.

Is This Your Style of Comedy?

One-Liners Comedians

Mitch Hedberg

Gary Delaney

Milton Jones

Tim Vine

Steven Write

Jimmy Carr

Demetri Martin

Note: In my comedy course, students often fear writing one-liner comedy. They think it's going to be far more challenging than it actually is.

Students are often surprised by how much they enjoy writing one-liners. Of course, real skill depends on how much time you spend writing. As with every other form of comedy, the more time you devote to practicing, the better you will become.

One-liner jokes are ideal for social media. They take skill but, once mastered, they can bring a gig to new heights.

It's Your Turn! Take Between One to Two Hours to Complete This Exercise. Good Luck.

1. Choose a few of the comedians from the one-liner list. Watch the YouTube clips, a full show, or even better, try and see them live.

2. Try writing some one-liner comedy. Aim to have five one-liner jokes before you finish for the day.

3. Write a Twitter joke (maximum 280 characters at the time of publishing). Comedians often try out their gags on Twitter. Posting on Twitter will help you with brevity and editing, as you'll need to restructure and take out unnecessary words.

Check-in: How did you find it? Would you like to write more jokes in this comedy style?

Improv Comedy

By improv, I mean the stand-up style, not the *Have I Got News For You* panel-show type.

Within stand-up, improv means being spontaneous with your audience during the delivery of your material.

You'll notice certain audience responses and reactions will come up time and time again. You can craft responses that, to onlookers, will look like improv. Situations like these can cover anything from audience members coming in late/using their phones, to hecklers shouting from the crowd.

If I could give one piece of advice to my students, it would be to start improv early on in your career. It will sharpen your skills considerably.

Google: ***Dara O Briain, This is the Show*** **-** The full show is excellent, though it's around the eight-minute mark you'll see a fine example of improv. **Watch it Before Moving On.**

Check-in: What did you think? Dara is one of the best in the business at improvising with his audiences, and this always makes an entertaining show.

I'd recommend going to see him or at least reading his book *Tickling the English.* It offers excellent insight into the life of a gigging comedian on tour

Adlibbing

Adlibbing is improv of the riskiest kind. It's when a comedian comes up with their material on stage in front of a live audience.

It's an admirable skill if you can do it. I personally prefer to write most of my set before going on stage.

Adlibbing is best used when you have vast experience as a comedian. Even then, most comedians will fully flesh-out their set before committing it to stage.

It's challenging to use a live environment to discover your material, but I admire comedians who do. It takes nerves of steel and courage. I tend to adlib and chat with the audience more when compering.

My advice: If you're doing a five-minute set, factor in a full minute during your set for improv. Preferably, do so after you've delivered a sturdy piece of material. Start with open mic spots, then progress to all gigs once you have the experience.
Improv forces you to think on your feet. I can't recommend it enough.

Pros

- Interacting with an audience keeps them engaged.
- Each show will be different.
- You'll grow in confidence, especially as you get better. There's nothing like having an audience laugh at something you just made up on the spot.
- Thinking on your feet is the No. 1 way to sharpen your skills as a comedian.
- You'll develop skills to deal with hecklers.
- Banter with the audience can produce a tonne of new material that can be used again.
- You're less likely to get bored with the same set month after month.

- You'll create a unique comedy set which will never be replicated.

Cons

- Some audience members won't get involved no matter how hard you try. They may be scared you'll embarrass them or they'll embarrass themselves.

- It can give focus to humourless people or gobshites.

- It may be easy to lose control if you're inexperienced.

- Improv won't always produce the "funny."

- Audiences can start talking among themselves.

Tips for this Style of Comedy

You need to be quick on your feet. A good memory helps too, especially with audience participation.

You don't have to tie all audience interaction together at the end, though it's beautiful when done right. The audience loves it, and I think Dara O'Briain does it brilliantly.

Confidence and bounce-back are essential. Not everything you say is going to be comedy gold ... and that's okay. You're just working your funny bone, and you'll get better the more you do it.

Audience members are generally aware when a comedian is using improv, and they'll appreciate it. Anything remotely funny often gets a bigger laugh, as you've just come up with it.

Stay calm if a line drops, as it doesn't matter. Follow up with a gag you know works well to get the audience back on side.

There's more on this in *The Gig Didn't Go Well* chapter in the follow-up book, *The New Comedian's Handbook*.

The key is just to try it. It's for one minute. What damage could you possibly do?

Other Good Improv Comedians

Ross Noble

Al Murray

Kristen Wiig

Katherine Ryan

Lee Mack

Todd Barry

Russell Howard

Jason Byrne

Q. Do You Think This is Your Style of Comedy?

In Summary

So, we've looked at four different genres of comedy. Hopefully, this gives you a good idea of what's out there.

This is NOT for labeling purposes, as a lot of comedy covers more than one of these categories. Many comedians mix it up. For example:

- Billy Connolly uses storytelling as well as observational comedy.

- Eddie Izzard tells long, themed stories involving fantasy, observation, and improv.

- Ross Noble uses improv with observational.

When my students view these clips, many gravitate towards observational comedy.

I enjoy a comedy set which includes a selection of styles. The audience usually embraces everything the comedian does well - accents, funny walks, playing the banjo…

You may be dead set on one style of comedy, but I advise you to experiment. At this stage, you don't know what you're capable of and what will work best for you.

It's Your Turn! Take Between Thirty and Sixty Minutes to Complete This Exercise. Good Luck.

Below are five scenarios that could easily happen during your set.

Improv is about thinking on your feet, so imagine you're on stage when each of these scenarios happen. Write a response for each

- An audience member is talking too loudly.

- An audience member butts-in at your punchline.

- The compere forgets your name when introducing you.

- Someone in the front row gets up during your set.

Check-in: How did that go for you? Adlibbing can seem scary, but it's a vital skill. You'll get better the more you do it.

How did you find the last four writing exercises?

Did you find one easier than the others? Would you like to write more of one in particular?

Now that you're aware of comedy's different styles, get experimenting. See which style works best for you.

Your Comedy Style

As you can see, comedy is diverse and wide-ranging. I hope you're enjoying exploring the different styles of comedy and starting to realise the scope of possibilities for your comedy.

It's Your Turn! Take Between Thirty and Sixty Minutes to Complete This Exercise. Good Luck.

1. Write down what type of comedy to which you're most drawn and with what you'd like to experiment. The two can be different.

2. Choose a theme of your choice (or a topic from the list in the next chapter). Write **five minutes** of new comedy. Don't overthink it!

3. Edit and rehearse your piece.

4. Film the result and keep the footage.

Check-in: Are you noticing any progress with your writing? Perhaps not the quality (yet), but with your confidence and quashing the inner critic?

The more you write…
The Answer…
…the better chance you'll have of producing successful material.

Use this as your mantra.

Comedy Journey Case Study

Polly had just moved to Brighton to work for a small company when she came across the Brighton Comedy Course. She hadn't met many people and thought it would be a good way to cure the boredom and meet some like-minded folks.

Polly said, "I'm one of those people who will never really do anything unless I have a lot of instruction/nagging/pushing or whatever happens to be available at the time. Without all the training, there is no way in a decade of Sundays I would have stood in front of a crowd and tried to be funny. The training was invaluable. It was also an incredible amount of fun, and I wish I could do it all again."

Polly preferred the practical aspects of the course, though acknowledged the best results come because of knowing theory.

One of the first things Polly said in class was, "I hate public speaking!" Following that, she stated, "I would rather eat a maggoty haggis than go on stage."

Her comfort level changed during the course. The main thing Polly gained was confidence.

"I will say sorry for breathing too loudly. I mean, I'll still say sorry now, but only if someone comments on it first (which never happens). The tuition was brilliant! I had been in creative writing and acting courses before where we were taught to write and act in ways. Of course, we were penalised if we didn't adhere to the tutor's vision. Louise encouraged every student to explore a variety of styles until they got into their stride."

I asked Polly if she had any advice for new comedians.

"One of the best things I learned in the course had been the art of the spider diagram. It's a simple technique that gets creative juices flowing. I still use it every time I want to change up my routine. Such a simple brainstorming technique … but I'd be lost without it."

Of the comedy circuit, Polly says, "Working on the circuit can be trying. If you have a good gig, you feel indestructible for days. A lousy gig, however! The most challenging thing is bouncing back after a tough gig. Some audiences would rather watch the tumbleweed go by than laugh at your joke. Five minutes can feel like forever when you're dying on your arse. The best thing to do is watch the video footage and get back on the horse as soon as possible. Licking your wounds won't get you anywhere. A few weeks "off" could quickly turn to months and then years if you let it.

When I have a good gig, it feels like I could win a dance-off against God. I feel as if there's electricity in my blood, and I'm hungry to do more. There's no other feeling like it in the world!

I've met loads of fabulously funny people. I treat gigs like classroom lessons. You're on stage, sure, but it's also a chance to learn from people who have much more experience and are possibly much funnier than you.

In my experience, the best moment so far was when a lady ran up to me after a gig and yelled, 'WHY HAVEN'T I SEEN YOU BEFOOOORE?'

That was nice!"

On graduation night, Polly recalls sweating so much it filtered through her deodorant, and she worried she'd look like she wet herself!

"When a pint was within reach, I wanted to down it. Fortunately, my lovely mum and sister had come to watch my debut, so they physically restrained me.

After the gig, I felt like I had been on fire. I was happy everyone had smashed it, and the atmosphere within the group had been terrific! Best of all, I no longer had a sweaty bum. It's all in the little things."

I asked Polly if anything has surprised her about comedy.

"You can make ANYTHING funny if you think about it enough. I know there are some 'shock' comedians out there, and I don't mean it in that way.

I mean, you can make opening a bottle of water funny. Or sitting on a chair in a certain way. There's comedy everywhere if you know where to look."

Polly intends to continue with stand-up comedy.

"It's still way too early to say I've found my comedy 'voice,' if such a thing exists, but without Louise's instruction, I'd still be gaping into a mic and telling 'Knock, Knock' jokes.

I'm lucky, as Brighton is a real comedy hub with plenty of open mic nights. I'll carry on until ten people tell me to stop. Even then, they'll all have to do it *en masse*, or I just won't listen!"

How to Source Material

Now that you're getting into the swing of things, you'll notice there's material everywhere! On TV, public transport, at home, at work, in the pub ... The subjects for comedy are limitless.

Even your name can be used as material. My name is 'Louise,' which means "woman warrior" and my surname is 'Stevenson,' which means "royalty."

"Royal warrior;" that's me. It's hard to believe when I wake up dribbling with half a kebab on my pillow!

Here are a few suggestions for comedy topics:

Television shows can be a great source of material. Shows generally work best when they're widely watched like *The X Factor.*

If you choose a more obscure show, that's fine. Make sure to give the audience some background on the show in a few sentences to make sure everyone's on the same page.

Using an exciting fact or survey is often an excellent way to generate material.

In 2011, an international survey was taken in which forty-eight countries voted the UK as one of the most promiscuous countries in the world! Google is a brilliant tool for coming up with material.

Use a search engine to ask any number of things. Whenever I do a gig in a new city, I Google "Ten Things About [Insert City] That People Don't Know."

Recently, I booked a corporate gig for an IT company. I Googled, "Things You Don't Know About IT Workers."
One fact that stood out to me was that 89% of IT workers don't tell their family or friends their profession for fear of being asked for help.

While that (probably) isn't true, it will get a laugh. Be creative with Google.

Nostalgia always goes down well with audiences.
As youngsters, we would record music off the radio and try to cut it off before the presenter started talking. (It was a real art and, once again, I'm showing my age.)

Tech is a No. 1 way to generate nostalgic comedy ideas - from old TV models and shows, music systems, computer games, soda streams, and more.

Food that speaks to your childhood works well too. Findus' Crispy Pancakes is a good one. Another example is when Spaghetti Bolognaise became a brand-new concept in the UK.

Peter Kay integrates nostalgia into his comedy brilliantly. It may be why he's got such a wide range of fans. Sixteen-year-olds and ninety-year-olds alike love his comedy.

There's something hugely funny about the old days, especially when compared to the present.

Politics. Many comedians have made a career from political material.

Politics is not my favorite topic, as it can date fast, but I've seen it elicit huge laughs from audiences.

Topical material can bring easy wins, like anything to do with Trump or Brexit.

Let me be clear. Political material is great; political rants are not.

A severe political rant will dampen the comedy atmosphere immediately. If you can't make it funny, steer clear.

The room you're gigging in. Acknowledging the room will make you sound more grounded.

Is it cold in the room in which you're performing? Are there weird posters on the walls?

One of my graduates had a gig in a church. A twenty-foot crucifix stood behind him. When he got on stage, he said: *"I said to the promoter, 'I will not work unless someone brings me a twenty-foot crucifix of Jesus Christ.'"*

Note of caution: If the venue is rough, it may not go down well with the regulars if you call it a shithole. Avoid saying anything negative if you want to gig there again.

These are just a few topic ideas. Be creative and write subjects attractive to you.

There are times when I'm chuckling away at my material. That's not a definitive sign of success, but you **must find your jokes funny.** If you don't, the audience won't either.

You may have heard the expression, "Write what you know." I don't necessarily agree with this. If you're writing about being a baker by trade, but you're not a baker by trade, that may bring a new level of difficulty.

If you don't have real-life experience with a topic, you may struggle to reach any depth. However, I've written material on things about which I've known nothing. (Thanks, Google!) Research and ask as many questions as you can, and you'll see you don't have to know everything about every topic you aim to write about.

In the comedy course, I do quick-fire rounds, giving each student a subject about which to write.

I often give my students subjects they'd never choose themselves. They regularly surprise themselves by having something funny to say about such topics.

Here's a list of ideas for writing material.

Your name
Shows on television- X Factor, the Apprentice- well watched
An interesting fact or survey e.g. in 2008 an international survey in 48 countries identified the UK as one of the most promiscuous countries.
Your environment- the room, the area. A city, e.g. where you're from or live now.
Topical current affairs
Your family or upbringing
Your partner/boyfriend
Do you have a Unique Selling Point-Your characteristics e.g. Scottish, small, height, big nose (success not dependant on this though it quite often work).
Characterises of where you grew up, Glasgow deep fried mars bars.
What annoys you?
What makes you happy?
Your job

Your travels
What happened the last night out you were drunk?
An incident- a night out, a wedding
Weather, winter, summer
Special shared events, Halloween, Xmas
Strange news stories
Instances of stupidity
Job descriptions
Advertisements
Celebrities

The list is not exhaustive. There is comedy all around you; just keep your eyes open and a pad nearby.

It's Your Turn! Take Between Thirty and Sixty Minutes to Complete This Exercise. Good Luck!

Choose a topic from the above list and write a five-minute set. Remember, it doesn't have to be hilarious right away, but it could be the foundation for something.

It's up to you if you want to use the spider chart to generate ideas first or if you're going to dive straight in.

Subjects That Don't Work

Skilled comedians can make most subjects funny, as they're experts at judging angles. However, if you inadvertently offend an audience, you can lose them entirely.

When I first started stand-up, women talking about their periods was a BIG no-no. However, a guy talking about his dick for twenty minutes was okay. Meh.

I figured talking about your period hadn't been original, so I steered clear. Then I saw a gig in Brighton where the female comedian did a cracking set on how a man would treat a period. (He ended up in the hospital, of course.) It was a great gag. Whether or not a piece such as this will work depends on the quality of the material and how the comedian delivers it.

Political Correctness

Some cities are more politically correct than others. Audience sensitivity varies.

When you've achieved the all-important first gig and have started working the comedy circuit, try to watch a gig in the area in which you're due to perform. If that's not possible, reach out to the local comedians on comedy forums. Try and gauge their levels of political correctness.

When you're working as a comedian, turn up to the gigs early. You'll be able to tell from the compere/audience interaction how sensitive the audience is.

As a rule, however, treat any given subject with a degree of sensitivity and respect.

I remember gigging in London on the night of 9/11. I'd never felt less like being funny. I'd spent the whole day horrified and in tears, so gigging was the last thing I wanted to do.

But I was booked, so I went. The compere, who shall remain nameless, mentioned the attack. In my head, I was begging him not to do it.

He said, "*I can really identify with the grief and trauma those people are dealing with today. I broke my nail this morning. It was a real bugger.*"

It was in terrible taste, and the audience's silence spoke volumes.

It's fine to use comedy to make a point, but don't be offensive just for its sake.

I know some comedians make a career using shock-tactics.

Some do it well and have a vast following. It just depends on what kind of comedian you want to be.

I've laughed hard at comedy with a victim, fictional or not, but I don't enjoy a laugh at a weak victim's expense. Also, I can't bear an audience's forced laughter - when they feel they need to laugh to lighten the room or because they're embarrassed.

In my experience, this is what I've found:

- Sport and comedy don't mix. There are too many different supporters, and a lot of people take the televised competition seriously. You don't want the audience to start pitting against one another.

- Subjects like pedophilia, rape, and cancer are best avoided.

- Jokes about race (not racist jokes) can work well e.g., more sophisticated versions of the Scottish, English, and Irish jokes to which you may have grown-up listening.

- Picking on people perceived as "weaker" than you will lose support. It's a real turn off for the audience. Avoid making fun of anyone for being fat, disabled, gay, or of an ethnic minority.

It's Your Turn! Take Between Thirty and Sixty Minutes to Complete This Exercise. Good Luck.

Think about a time you've seen some comedy (live or on TV) and it hasn't worked. Ask yourself: What was the audience's reaction? Is there something the comedian could have done better? How can you tell when an audience is not reacting well to a piece of material?

Structuring Material

There are a few ways I set out my material, which I find incredibly useful when writing.

- I always type my material. Typing makes editing easy, and, if the set needs restructuring, rearranging text is simple.

- I write my content in paragraphs. This helps define each joke.

- I underline the main topic of each section to help me remember the order of the set.

- When I complete my first draft, I write a bullet-point list of the items I've underlined. Again, these tips help me to remember the order of the set. The raving days were hard on my memory.

Openers and Closers

I structure my comedy set so I start and finish with a strong gag. These are called openers and closers.

Always open with a gag. A good opening line will get you your first laugh.

Once you have your first laugh, you and the audience will relax, as they'll feel as if they're in safe hands.

This is your introduction to the audience, so grab their attention. You can save long set-ups for later in the gig.

Opening lines also help establish who you are.

Useful opening lines could be:

- A characteristic about you.
- The premise of your gig or your first bit of material.
- An observation about the audience or venue.
- A representation of how your feeling or what happened to you today.
- Something unpredictable and surprising also works. I once saw a seventy-year-old woman be assisted to the stage. She started her set by saying how much she loves sex!

There are endless subjects with which to open your gig. Below is one of my favorites:

The fantastic Stu Francis, the Canadian comedian we looked at for our one-liner comedy, started his set on British TV by stating the obvious: *"Don't worry, I've not heard of you either."*

It's Your Turn! Take Between Thirty to Sixty Minutes to Complete This Exercise. Good Luck.

1. List as many "state-the-obvious" opening lines of which you can think - one after another.

2. Use the spider chart and put your name in the middle. Flesh it out with your characteristics, personality, quirks, loves, and hates. What do your mates say about you? What about your boss?

3. Look at the chart and write as many one-liners as possible, taking inspiration from these ideas.

Check-in: How did you get on? Got a few you like?

Openers are great with which to experiment. When you're working on the circuit, you'll experience the impact a good opener can make.

Be as "out there" as you like. If you connect with the audience and get a laugh straight away, it's full speed ahead.

Closing Lines

You want to end on a high note. It's what your audience will remember. So, keep it sharp.

Again, you have endless possibilities. You could use:

- One of your personal characteristics you listed earlier.
- A thread (also known as a call-back) from a bit of material you used earlier in your gig.
- A "part of the process" gag. E.g.*"If you liked me, then... If you didn't, then..."*
- A summary of you or your act.
- The moral of the story
- A play on your name which will make the audience. remember it (often used in the U.S.)

One of My Favorite Closing Lines, Again by Stu Francis

"I have to go. I'm late for Actor's Anonymous. I have to be there in ... [exaggerates as he checks his watch] *two hours!"*

You've seen Stu's opening and closing one-liners now. Don't copy from other comedians.

Make sure your opener is original and unique to you; though do keep a list of the ones you like from other comedians. Something may resonate and could help you mold your own opening and closing lines for the future.

It's Your Turn! Take Between Thirty and Sixty Minutes to Complete This Exercise. Good Luck.

Write a closing line using the suggestions above. Try as many as possible.

If you already have a set, see how these gel with the rest of your material.

Check-in: So, you've now written an opening and closing line. Well done.

You will likely chop and change these over the years. Writing opening lines is a great short exercise you can do whenever you have half an hour.

This process also works as an exercise to help you write new comedy material.

Joke Structure

Traditionally, a joke's structure is in two parts: the set-up and the punchline.

The set-up creates an expectation, and the punchline reveals the surprise.

Try and get into the habit of structuring your material in this format:

- Short sentences.
- Double-spaced lines for editing.
- New paragraphs for each joke.

A typical joke structure is a two-line build-up, then a punchline.

Here are a few bits from my material, for example:

1. "Has anyone been to Glasgow? (Audience participation)
   Did you get beat up or mugged? (Audience participation)
   No, you didn't get off the coach, did you? Just drove straight through."

2. "I went to India, though I didn't manage to find myself. What I did find was a whole new way of releasing food at an astonishing rate... Dehli Belly."

That's the crux of the joke, though you can add a line like:

"I completely lost the confidence to fart!"

You can have lots of jokes on one subject.

Try and keep a three-line subject. A three-line subject will help sharpen your jokes and prompt you to make your set-up lines funnier.

It will also help you remember your jokes on stage if you use a sequence such as this.

One-Liner Jokes

One-liners can stand alone or help support a subject. They should be short and to the point.

1. "My wife and I decided we don't want children. If anyone does, we can drop them off tomorrow."
   Stu Francis

2. "Glasgow is the only place in the world where Tourette Syndrome is seen as a gift." Louise Stevenson

Two-Line Jokes

1. "All bad things come in threes. Atomic Kitten."
   Jimmy Carr

2. "Old people, you can't beat them. Pity!" Peter Kay

The purpose of the first draft of your material is to flesh out ideas. It's okay to have excess words and sentences, as long as they're removed in the editing process.

Excess words slow down the momentum of material. Editing is a skill which becomes natural with practice.

It's Your Turn! Take Between Thirty and Sixty Minutes to Complete This Exercise. Good Luck.

Take a piece of your favourite material and edit it to remove excess words.

Are there any full sentences that don't add anything to the punchline?

Write your material in the format above: short sentences with paragraphs for each section.

Check-in: In the writing world, it's called "killing your darlings."

Print out your material and read it aloud. This way, you'll be able to identify what's slowing down your set. Editing **makes** your content the best it can be.

Remember the stages of comedy writing:

- Writing
- Editing
- Performing aloud

Editing Material

To recap: Good editing can make the difference between a hilarious set and a bad one.

Keep your material punchy. Don't babble or add sentences that don't add anything to the punchline.

I've seen many students do impressions of me, repeating: *"Keep it punchy, keep it punchy."*

As a rule of thumb, aim for three to five punchlines (which should equal laughs) per minute of your set. Don't panic. People starting out may not have three to five per minute, but it's a good aim. If a sentence doesn't add anything to your material, take it out. I wrote material about a trip I had to India some years ago. Here's a look at before and after the edit.

Before

You like my tan? I went to Goa in India this year in the summer. It's so nice. People go there to find themselves. I didn't manage to find myself. What I did manage to find was a whole new way to release food at an astonishingly quick rate, Dehli Belly. It was horrible, both sides. Extremely disgusting. I completely lost the confidence to fart!

After

I went to India; I didn't manage to find myself. What I did manage to find was a whole new way to release food at an astonishingly quick rate, Dehli Belly. It was horrible, both sides. I completely lost the confidence to fart!

Can you see the difference? Notice how I've removed the surplus words and sentences that don't contribute anything to the joke? I removed twenty-two words from the first edit. If you tend to be overly wordy, watch out when writing comedy. It can slow down a joke.

Note: When you're writing new material, don't worry about editing. It's fine to follow a train of thought and write it down.

You can edit after. With practice you'll see what sentences need to go.

It's Your Turn! Take one Hour to Complete This Exercise. Good Luck.

Find your favorite piece of material and try these editing techniques:

- Read over your content.
- Underline any bits upon which you want to expand.
- Write down any other ideas that come to mind.
- Are there any obvious "filler" sentences? If so, take them out.

When to Edit & When to Ditch Material

When students start on the circuit, they ask: "Should I ditch any material that doesn't get a laugh?"

I try to rework material before I dump it. I mean, I obviously thought the subject was funny enough to write about in the first place.

There's an ace bit of advice from Dara O'Briain in his book *Tickling the English*. He says, "[Editing] is like stripping an engine and putting it back together again."

When you're rehearsing, or when you're actually out there doing the job, look back on (watch a recording of) your performance and ask yourself: What does it need? Would it work better earlier or later in the set?

Ask fellow comedians who you trust to review your material, but only if you're prepared to listen to their response.

I try out a joke three times before shelving it. Remember, your best material will be the stuff you know well. The more familiar you are with it, the better you'll deliver the content.

Comedy content evolves and gets funnier as you get more intimate with it. If it's not working, shelve it for a while and go back to it at a later stage.

Performance & Stage Techniques

Until now, the focus of this book has been on writing and editing material. You should now have plenty of material to perform.

As I said before, if you can get used to splitting your allotted comedy time into three parts, it will see you well.

If I dedicated six hours a week to my comedy, I would:

- Write for two hours
- Edit for two hours
- Rehearse aloud for two hours

If your material is brilliant but your performance isn't, you will be let down.

Generally, performance is tied to confidence. The more you perform, the better you'll be; and the more stage time you have, the more your confidence will grow. It's as simple as that.

I was a completely different comedian on my thirtieth gig in comparison to my tenth. And there was an even greater difference on my hundredth gig compared to my thirtieth.

Keep working the stages and take the time to evaluate what jokes are successful.

Mic, Mic Stand, and Performance Tips:

- When the compere calls your name to take the stage, take a deep breath. This will help you relax, so your voice will find its natural level. It will also slow you down (which is a good thing)!

- Ground yourself. Position the mic the way you want it, and don't rush.

- Relax your shoulders. Pulling them up near your ears shows you are nervous.

- Pause before you speak. Look at your audience, make eye contact, and smile. Make the smile look natural. Grimaces are less funny and more horror-movie.

- Pausing to take a drink makes you appear confident. It also allows you to take stock of your audience. Don't overdo it though.

- Change the focus of your eye contact during your performance. Staring at one person can be a bit disconcerting and odd. Likewise, the audience wants to feel a connection with you. Share the love.

- Sometimes the stage lights can blind you, and you'll only see the front row. The trick is to make everyone feel like you can see them.

- A little walking around on stage is okay, but not too much. Pacing makes you look nervous, and it's distracting.

- Keep your voice relaxed. Don't speak too quickly or mumble. You'll lose your audience.

- Keep your tone even. Shrieking is never fun to listen to, and it's worse in a mic.

- Some comedians like to use a mic stand. It's a good grounding prop if you tend to pace around. I want to move, so I take the mic out of the stand. If you're not using the stand, put it behind you and out of the way.

- Keep the mic a few inches away from your mouth. If you hold it too close, it'll produce "pah" noises, which are distracting. It's also not hygienic to put your mouth too close to the mic.

- Many venues have cordless mics, which will offer the flexibility of movement. If you're working with a wired mic, make sure it's not tangled in the stand. Take your time. Not hurrying shows confidence.

- Always perform a mic check at gigs. The compere usually does this at the start of a gig.

- Try not to fiddle with the mic's "On/Off" switch. Pay attention to the compere to see if there's feedback in certain corners of the room. If so, tell the compere or tech person.

Performance Tips

- If you are in front of a small audience, you can get off the stage to be closer to them. Just make sure everyone can still see you.

- If it's dark in the room and there's a stage light, you may have to remain on stage to be seen.

- Show some human frailty. Among the bravado and self-confidence, throw in some self-deprecation. Audiences like to know you have your feet on the ground.

- Act out dialogue when you change characters. E.g. If acting out a conversation between two characters in a set, swap positions and add a different voice, accent, or facial expression. Maybe even add a prop like a hat or a cigarette. **Don't** use a prop that's too unwieldy.

- Don't use too much preamble as it just wastes time. If it doesn't contribute to a joke, remove it. On a similar note, you don't need to tell the audience when you wrote the joke. The audience doesn't care. Just bring the funny.

- If you go on stage and say, "I haven't got anything new," or "Sorry, I've not had time to work on this," you can count on one unimpressed audience. It's like saying to a teacher you haven't done your homework.

- Don't perform if you're not prepared.

Note: You don't need to follow all these tips right away, but it's good to be professional from the start. If you want to perform stand-up as a job, then treat every gig as one.

A previous comedy graduate contacted me to say how shocked he was when so many acts went on stage unprepared. He was grateful he'd learned excellent organisational skills in the course. As a result, he was more confident and had a better rapport with the audience than a lot of the more experienced comedians on the bill.

I have to say, I was chuffed with the feedback. Moral of the story: Prepare, Prepare, Prepare.

It's Your Turn! Take Between Thirty and Sixty Minutes to Complete This Exercise. Good Luck.

Spend one hour performing your material while employing the techniques above. You can practice in front of the mirror with a hairbrush. Buy a cheap mic if it helps you get into it more.

You might feel like an eejit at the beginning, but it'll soon wear off. There are so many benefits to rehearsing your material aloud.

Your timing and intonation will improve, which will further enhance your delivery. We'll dive into this in more detail later.

Comedians often record their rehearsals on their phones and watch them back. If you find this harrowing, just record the audio. Whatever works for you.

Be analytical. Don't just collect the footage. Afterwards, decide what would make it better? Does it need more emphasis on a certain line?

Did you talk too quickly? Mumble? Would adding actions or body language improve the joke?

Have you made the joke work better before? Why?

Deconstruct bits which aren't working well for you on and off the stage.

Joke Tactics and Formulas

Joke formulas work well with audiences, but they should be used sparingly.

As soon as an audience starts to predict your punchlines, they become less effective.

That said, formulas are fun to play around with. Writing straight material is fine, but experiment with these and see what you come up with.

The Comparison Joke

The comparison joke is exactly what it says on the tin. You're comparing two things for comedy effect. Again, use this formula in moderation, or it can become predictable.

"Brexit is a lot like Twitter: There are 140 characters, and bad things are constantly happening."

Obviously, the audience must be familiar with Brexit and Twitter to appreciate the joke.

They will recognise Brexit has a large cast of characters without stopping to think about the terrible things happening on Twitter. Basically, they won't dissect the joke if it works.

Here's another type of comparison joke:

I like my men like my alcohol. Cold, cheap, and nasty.

I like my men like my food. Hot, spicy, and well-proportioned.

"Men are like dolphins - best enjoyed on holiday!"
Katherine Ryan

The Surprise Element

Comedy relies on surprise. It can be an unexpected comparison like the above or humorous observation.
Below is an example of a play on words using the surprise element:

"A bus station is where the bus stops. A train station is where the train stops. On my desk, I have a workstation."
William Faulkner

Or you've got the misleading set-up:

"I want to die peacefully in my sleep, like my grandpa. Not screaming and yelling like the passengers in his car."
Will Rogers

If you can make the audience predict the rest of the sentence, then pull the rug from under their feet, you've got a good joke. Or you could rework some popular sayings. For example:

"I'm so hungry, I could ride a horse." Chris, Family Guy

"Don't judge a book by its movie." Popular T-Shirt Slogan

Rule of Three

Grouping items into three can have a satisfying pay-off.

The first element introduces the idea, the second reinforces it, and the third deviates from what's expected from the audience.

"Suppose you were an idiot. Now suppose you were a member of Congress. But I repeat myself." Mark Twain

"I got my first bikini. It's a three-piece: It's a top, a bottom, and a blindfold for you." Wendy Liebman

Pull Back and Reveal

"Pull back and reveal" is a term derived from the TV practice of panning out from a close-up shot to a broader picture.

In comedy, you are holding back a piece of pertinent information until the end of the story.

In the wrong hands, this is a common and predictable technique. Cliched punchlines include: "Then I got off the bus," and "That was just the teachers!"

But if there's skill behind it, it can be sublime. One of my favorite openers is from a disheveled Michael Redmond:
"People often say to me ... get out of my garden."

Puns

Puns aren't everyone's bag. Most puns are somewhat corny and obvious. Although, if you're entirely unashamed, it can be infectious.

Here's one from Tim Vine:

'I've decided to sell my Hoover. It was just collecting dust."

It's Your Turn! You'll need a Few Hours to Complete This Exercise. Good Luck.

1. Try writing a comparison joke. Come up with ten and post your favorite one to Twitter (or another social media platform) if you're confident enough to get constructive (or other) feedback.

2. Write a joke using the Rule of Three. Don't forget the surprise element! Come up with three (hahaha) and test your favorite on a friend or family member.

3. Write three jokes using the "Pull Back and Reveal" set-up. Share the best one with someone using the delivery techniques you've learned so far.

Check-in: How did you find these writing techniques?

These formulas may take more effort to write than writing other material. However, they will become more natural with practice and will hopefully have satisfying payoffs. They're great for getting the creative juices flowing, and they generally don't take too long to write.

Comedy Journey Case Study

When Russell joined the comedy course, he was a mature student who'd just finished an Arts Practice PhD, which was a discussion about using humour. He was writing an academic article about using satire and humour in educational contexts.

He delivers hilarious material on The Dull Man's Club, with an agenda of hot issues like how to crush tin cans, where your favourite wall is, and "Can pigeons swim?" His deadpan delivery goes down a treat with his audiences.

Asked about his reasons for coming to a comedy course, Russell said, "I had a fear of performing, and I wanted to see if I could actually be funny on stage. The course was helpful in working towards my first stand up gig. Standing in front of people and attempting to get a laugh was, at first, slightly overwhelming. After several weeks I gradually became less anxious, allowing me to connect more with the audience. The course allowed for experimentation and finding my comedy feet but, especially in the final weeks, the focus was firmly on building toward the actual gig."

On graduation night, Russell knew his material inside out, which he felt reduced his nerves. "My first joke had worked well in practice and got a good response on the night. The laughter from the audience was great. Afterwards I felt like I'd really achieved something."

Russell enjoyed the theory of the course and learning about the different styles and the technicalities of doing stand-up, but he enjoyed the practical element most. "Having a safe space to practice and develop a comedy set was the main thing. We had a supportive group, and this made it a real collective journey."

Russell has kept up momentum since finishing the course and has been working the comedy circuit in Brighton and London. Working the circuit has developed into his main interest. "The course has made me more daring, and the experience has helped generally with expressing my views and not taking life too seriously."

"It was remarkable value for money. Louise goes the extra mile and keeps everything bubbling along, both during and after the official group meetings. After the course had finished, Louise remained supportive and made sure people had gigs if they wanted to continue. I've met a lot of funny people and it's got an anarchic edge.

I'm interested in producing good material and getting it out there, so its enjoyable to experiment. As I keep going, I'm gradually improving and learning the ropes. I've had some comedy competition success, and I've met a whole community of performers I knew next to nothing about."

On the topics of the comedy circuit and gigs, Russell said, "The comedy circuit can be challenging, some nights are great and then other nights there's little audience, and all the acts need to soldier on. I've had gigs, however, where everyone laughed lots.

My performance at a well-known venue in London received a good response; it was daunting passing the pictures of famous comedians who'd performed there on the way to the stage. Afterwards, it was nice when more professional acts said I'd done very well."

Russell plans to keep working on his comedy. He's not just a comedy talent but a thoroughly nice man (and not dull at all)! Watch out for this fella.

Confidence, Comfort Zone, and Mindset

Confidence plays a huge part in the success of a comedian.

If you can bring confidence to your performance, you've won half the battle.

When I watch a confident comedian take the stage, I relax. Their material may not be fabulous, but their confidence reassures me they have faith in what they're doing.

Confidence has an impact on delivery, timing, and the overall quality of a gig. Confident comedians won't crumble when the odd joke doesn't work. They're less fearful about a joke falling on its arse.

I love the following quote: *"Comfort is the enemy of progress."*

You get five points if you can tell me from where I found it? (The prize here is knowledge).

It's from *The Greatest Showman.*

What is a Comfort Zone?

A comfort zone is a self-imposed limitation. It's something we've given ourselves!

Moreover, as it's something we've given ourselves, we can always expand it. Aim to stretch yourself both on and off the stage.

Why Do People Stay in Their Comfort Zone?

People stay in their comfort zones mainly for fear of failure and rejection. Most people assume others are more confident than they are.

My story would be awfully different if I hadn't found the confidence to push myself into uncharted territory.

When I was young, I was a bit of a tomboy. I hung around in a group of ten to fifteen kids, mostly lads. We often played football after school.

I was always in goal, but I KNOW I could have been a great midfielder if given a chance.

I remember funny lines popping into my head and not having the confidence to say them out loud. I did start speaking up at school and became the class clown. It was my first taste of having an audience, and I loved it!

Eventually, it became easier to speak up and say what came to mind. However, I bet my teachers would have preferred me to be in my box … or a box underground.

Someone recently said to me, *"You must have people on your comedy course with no sense of humour."*

I thought about it and disagreed. I believe everyone has a sense of humour, but confidence plays a massive part when trying to find it.

There's a line from The Smiths' popular song *Ask,* which talks about how being shy can stop you doing things in life that you want to.

They make a good point. We need to put ourselves out there if we want to succeed.

The first time we do something new, we often wrestle with self-doubt. We question ourselves: *"Will I embarrass myself? Do I really want to do this?"*

But then, think how much easier it becomes the second time around ... and the third time.

Your Mindset and Perception

People tend to assume that others are more confident than they are.

Researchers uncovered something called the *Confidence Con.* The Confidence Con is the scientifically verified tendency for people to over-attribute the confidence of others.

If someone looks comfortable(ish), we assume they're much more confident than we are.

Have you heard of *Transparency Bias?* Transparency Bias is when we think our shortcomings are clearly on display, even when they're not. This naturally causes self-doubt and insecurity.

So, part of the problem is pure perception. We assume people are more confident than they are, and we imagine our own feelings of insecurity are more visible.

When you recognise these things aren't real, you've overcome a huge barrier. This recognition opens so much potential to us on and off-stage.

When clients come to the comedy course or the first 1-2-1 coaching session, I can see the fear etched on their faces.
Then I watch them do their first gig and come off stage with huge smiles, beaming with confidence.

It's my favorite thing about being a comedy coach.

You have the potential to be confident. Remember the expression, *"You're a long time dead,"* and let that confidence shine in life.

It's Your Turn! Take an Hour to Complete This Exercise. Good Luck.

1. Write down five aspirations that you would complete if your confidence allowed it.

2. Don't overthink it. Look down the list and choose at least one of those aspirations on which to follow through. Decide on a timeframe and write down the steps it will take to complete the task.

3. Rate your confidence on a scale of one to ten. Write the number down in your diary. Recheck the figure in two to three months to see if it's the same. (It won't be!)

Check-in: Have you got a plan?

Expand your comfort zone and go into new territory. (Unless you're considering mass murder … Just don't.)

Take your newfound confidence far and wide. You can do it! X

(It took courage to put that kiss (X) there. I wasn't sure it was professional. I did it anyway because I wanted to PUSH my confidence levels). Yeah me!

Harness Nerves & Find the Right Headspace

Nerves don't have to be a negative thing.

Nervousness is excitement. It's butterflies in your belly.

Nerves supply the adrenaline needed for a good gig. We should embrace them. You will get the best out of your gig if you can learn to harness nervous excitement.

You've heard the expression, "*Fake it 'til you make it.*"

Hide your nerves and follow the performance tips I've given you. These will help you look more confident.

When you take to the stage, pause and position your mic so you're comfortable. Put your drink down and smile at the audience (as naturally as possible.) Don't forget to put the mic stand behind you if you're not using it.

Don't hold paper. I'm not a fan of comedians going on stage with notes. If you're nervous and you have shaky hands, the audience will notice it.

Avoid mumbling. If nerves make you stumble over certain words, swap them out for ones easier to pronounce.

Here are tips to help give you an extra layer of confidence.

Mentally

- Have a "backup thought" or mantra. These can vary significantly from comedian to comedian. My backup thought is, *"This audience doesn't know me or give a shit about me or my life."* I find this thought allows me to drop my shoulders and breathe easier.

- Remember, this time tomorrow, your gig will be over. It'll be back to everyday life (which, as you know, can lack excitement at times).

- Know your material. When I go on stage, I know my stuff inside and out. This makes me more confident and works miracles to keep my nerves in check. I think, "*I worked hard on my writing, editing, and rehearsing for this gig. I'm confident I know what I'm delivering*".

- This gives me room to have fun with the audience, allowing me to build a personal connection with them. I'm also more confident if there are interruptions or hecklers because they can't throw me off.

- Keep in mind it's okay for new comics to mess up. It's not the end of the world. Your patient won't die. You won't bankrupt the nation.

- The early years of comedy are great, as there's little to no expectations at open mic spots. You won't lose an agent, TV audience, money, or credibility at this stage because **you don't yet have any**. Yippee. Freedom.

Physically

- Arrive at the gig in plenty of time. There have been times, especially in big cities like London or Melbourne, when I've not given myself enough time to get there. I've been running down streets, sweating profusely, and asking people for directions. At the same time, I'm trying to call the promoter to let them know I'm running late as they might have to change the running order.

  It's **not** a good way to turn up to a gig. You'll also miss the opportunity to check out the room properly and listen to the compere and other comedians before you go on. Always have the promoter's contact details on your phone.

- Stretch! (Though I've not done this for years.) I'd stretch my calves before a gig. I found it comforting. I've never seen other comedians do it, but it works for me.

- Vocal exercises. I have an accent, as do we all, but performing with a Scottish accent abroad is challenging. I need to slow down so the audience can understand me. Saying a few sentences of my material slowly helps, as does mouthing the vowels A E I O U.

  Singers and actors often use similar techniques. Saying a few sentences aloud slowly lends itself to a much more natural speaking voice when it comes to performing.

- Relax your tongue in your throat and expand your sense of awareness.

- If your mouth is dry, take a glass of water or a drink on stage. Just make sure to put it somewhere solid and take it off the stage with you.

- Take everything one step at a time and breathe from your belly. As I mentioned previously, take a deep breath when the compere calls your name.

- Stage fright: In the twenty plus years I've been working on the stand-up circuit, I can't think of a single time where an act has got up on stage, said nothing, and got off. I imagine it's happened somewhere, but it's rare. You generally always remember your opening line.

  Get the first laugh and then go with it. There may be a

time when you can't remember the next bit of your routine, but generally, you can pull something to say out of the bag. If this ever happens, ask the audience a question to buy time.

If you need to change your mind-set on stage, then imagine everyone in the room owes you money and they've come to ask for an extension to pay.

It's Your Turn! Take A Minimum of Two Hours to Complete This Exercise. Good Luck.

1. Choose a topic from the subject list given in the "How to Source Material" chapter. Write, edit, and rehearse the material. Time it and aim for a five-minute set (which is standard for an opening spot in the UK and abroad).

2. Record a piece of your material and watch it back. Write down your thoughts in your notepad. What are you doing well? What needs improving? Do you look confident? Is your material punchy enough? Is your content well-edited and peppered frequently with punchlines?

Check-in: As you progress towards your first performance, you should start increasing your writing and rehearsing time.

Allow the exercises more time and put a few hours aside for writing material each week. If you can write daily, then do it. You'll be glad you put in the time. It'll give you the best chance of an enjoyable first gig, full of audience laughter.

The Thing about Audiences

Audiences are just people like you and me. They all have their own worries, flaws, and values.

Here's what's worth remembering about audiences:

- Most people want to laugh. They don't go to a comedy night to be miserable. They want to be cheered up, have fun, and laugh.

- Audiences want you to like them too! It's a two-way street, a relationship of sorts. They're wishing you well. You do well, and they get to laugh and be happy.

  There are exceptions. Clubs like "Up the Creek" in London encourage audiences to heckle. They use the "School of Hard Knocks" approach, and one has reached a milestone when doing well there. However, I'd avoid it until you have more experience.

- The more relaxed you are, the more relaxed your audience will be.

- Know your audience. A Sydney crowd is quite different from a Glasgow crowd. Tweak and edit your material for a specific audience. Throw in content about the town, landmarks, people, and the typical culture. In Brighton, a bisexual, cat-loving vegan is not unusual on Gumtree house-share ads.

- Remember, audience expectations won't be sky-high at an open mic gig.

- Audiences like a joke about someone in the audience they know and like. E.g., Big Ron, a local character, or that day's Birthday Boy, etc. Listen to your compere to find out more about your audience. Then, try to come up with a line about them before going on. This can win over an audience and involve them in your set.

Occasionally you can anticipate your audience, especially for corporate gigs or at members clubs. E.g. rugby guys - *"You've a big neck there, fella,"* etc. There will be general characteristics that'll get a laugh. Knowing your audience provides more opportunity for comedy and connection.

- Stand at the back of the room before you go on. Listen to the audience and get a feel for the place. Remember to watch your audience for success indicators during your own set.

Big No No's

- Don't insult a member of the audience harshly unless they heckle you harshly. You'll instantly lose audience support.

- Putting down an audience member weaker than you is another sure way of losing support.

- Don't keep asking the audience questions. It makes it harder to keep up momentum unless you're fabulous at improv.

- Don't show a shred of doubt in your performance. You can be self-deprecating about a bit of material but not your performance.

- Don't make a reference or draw attention to every joke that dies. It's funny once or twice. If you keep doing it though, you'll risk undermining your own set.

- Don't assume a home-crowd is a comfort zone.

- Don't expect a round of applause for naming the city in which you were raised. It's not *Blind Date*! (UK reference: A legendary program for finding love.)

- Don't make a habit of reading material or looking at notes on your hand. It halts momentum, and it's a bad habit. It looks unprofessional. It also shows you don't know your material.

  There are open mic nights where it's more acceptable, though it will affect the delivery and timing of your joke. Your content will NEVER be as good when you're reading.

It's Your Turn! This is a Three-Part task. Good Luck.

1. This writing exercise is called The Rant. Write down all the things which annoy you. It's often a long list. Take fifteen minutes and write as many annoyances as possible, no matter how petty.

2. Read your list. Which one stands out? Write five minutes of new material about it. This is a fun exercise. Remember, you can use your spider chart first if you want to flesh out your ideas. Enjoy.

Comedy Delivery

The combination of material, delivery, and timing are all internally linked and needed for a successful gig.

Delivery is a combination of body language, voice, tone, facial expressions, and pauses.

People sometimes get hung up on what comedic delivery is. Basically, it's *how you say your material.*

Chances are, if you're already funny and making friends and family laugh, you're already using your delivery skills.

Tips on Delivery

- Be confident.

- Try with different demeanors - serious, angry, scatty, confused. Try one piece of material with different attitudes and see what works.

- Study other comedians' delivery, but don't try to emulate them. That works for **their** humor. Your own kind of delivery will work for yours.

- Don't be monotone. Vary your voice.

- Exaggerate and match material with attitude. I occasionally witness comedians delivering content that apparently "outrages" them while smiling! They don't look outraged at all.

  Match your emotion to the situation you're describing, just as you would in real life. You wouldn't say "I am so excited and happy" while crying.

- If you have an accent, try to enunciate as much as possible.

- Speak loud enough for the audience to hear you without shouting.

- Signal your punchline by adding a little pause beforehand.

- Keep your shoulders back and open. Make eye contact with your audience.

- If a confused, angry, or surprised, expression adds more to your material, add it.

It's Your Turn! Take Between One and Two Hours to Complete this Exercise. Good Luck.

1. Watch two different comedians and make notes on their delivery techniques. What actions do they take to add to what they're saying? You can choose your favorite comedians or try someone new from the list provided in the genres of comedy chapters.

2. Look at a previous bit of material you think has potential. Edit it using the techniques you've learnt. Make it as punchy as possible.

Check-in: Have you upped your writing time?

Are you writing regularly?

If you were to aim for a date for your first performance, when would that be?

How to Deal with Hecklers

Comedy students often think the worst part about doing stand-up comedy is being heckled.

You'll be pleased to know heckling happens far less often than you think.

In twenty years, I've rarely been heckled (though the Glaswegian accent may have something to do with that. It can be quite intimidating when applied).

Most audiences are respectful. They've paid their money to be entertained.

That said, there'll be a few in the audience who think they could be much funnier than you. They'll try and get involved in the comedy as much as possible by shouting out and/or answering rhetorical questions.

This usually happens in bigger comedy clubs where they can hide amongst the crowd. A lot of the bigger clubs have security to prevent drunken hecklers from wrecking a show. Stag and Hen parties can be tricky!

Not all hecklers are bad. I've heard the occasional corker over the years that's made both the audience and comedian laugh their arses off.

When this happens, it's best to be humble and give them credit. As long as you are in control of the situation, just acknowledge the joke, thank the audience member, and move on.

One school of thought is that the heckler is a valuable member of the audience. They deserve to be entertained and respected, not insulted ... until he goes too far! Then you can attack from the moral high ground, safe in the knowledge he started it.

The other school of thought is that the heckler interrupted your set, so anything is fair game. It's down to you, the comedian, to decide on your approach.

I'm not particularly hard on hecklers, as I find it unnecessary. I'll put in one or two solid put-downs and move on.

However, I work with some comedians who will **annihilate** the heckler - much to the amusement of the audience.

Worth Noting about Heckling

There are fabulous heckle comebacks out there, but don't try and crowbar them into your set.

Don't spend too much time worrying or preparing for hecklers, as it rarely happens.

Write your own original comeback lines. Once you're on the comedy circuit, you'll hear the same comebacks repeatedly. Try to be unique.

Don't lose your temper on stage. Once you lose your temper, the gig is over. You're no longer an act. You're just an angry person with a mic.

My Favorite Heckler Gig

I was on a bill with Jimmy Carr at the Banana Cabaret comedy night in London.

A member of the audience was extremely drunk and had convinced himself he was hilarious. Jimmy **tore strips off him**. You could see the heckler's poor girlfriend sliding further and further under the table trying to hide. It was hilarious. The moral of the story is: Never heckle Jimmy Carr. He'll destroy you.

My Experience with Hecklers

I mentioned the "Up the Creek" comedy club in an earlier chapter.

This club encourages the audience to heckle and get involved. I was booked there in early 2000, and I had just been to a family funeral in Glasgow. When I arrived at the venue, a close friend of mine begged me not to go on after witnessing the carnage inside.

I was never more ready to deal with eejits that day. I was in no mood to take any shit. I went on stage, picked up a pint glass and, in my broadest of Glaswegian accent, said:

"Yes, I do have an accent. If anyone here doesn't understand what I'm saying, just put your hand up. [Scowl around the audience.] "When the glass reaches you, you'll know you've been acknowledged, and you can put your hand down!"

This did the trick, and I enjoyed the rest of the gig.

On another night, I gigged at a pub in Essex. It was a real drunken affair, and the audience was hammered. I was the only female on the bill, which wasn't unusual those days. It's a little better now, but I digress.

The gig wasn't going well, and within minutes of being on stage, a large numpty of a man shouted, "Get your tits out!"

(I know, this wasn't even in the Dark Ages.)

I looked him dead in the eye and said, "Why don't you save your breath to blow up your girlfriend later."

I thought I'd win the Hero Award and get the audience on side.

Nope.

It had the complete opposite effect because I had just insulted BIG JOHN.

There's a BIG JOHN in every pub, and everyone loves him.

My insult went down like a lead balloon. The audience was affronted on BIG JOHN'S behalf, regardless of him being a sexist pig.

I left the stage before my time was up, and I was **fuming.** I gave the audience a piece of my mind before I left the stage.

Learning Curve on This Gig

Had I been at the back of the room, rather than in the green room, I would have realised BIG JOHN was everyone's favorite arsehole.

Tips for Dealing with Hecklers

- Be brave and confident. If you have a no-nonsense look, then apply it.

- If the audience hears the heckler, then don't ignore it. Address it

- If it's come right at a crucial part of your set, then comment. Have a line about it. I've heard some great ones. Quite often they are based on a different kind of climax.

- Have a tough line you can use if you want to avoid a heckler. I say, "Yeah, feel free to heckle me, but keep in mind that I'm from Glasgow. I have a real propensity for violence." Only insult the real prats.

- If you repeat what the heckler says - They will often sound stupid, and the entire audience will hear what he/she said. It also buys you time to come up with something. Sometimes, however, just repeating it and throwing the audience a "Who is this guy?" look is enough.

- Remember, you're looking to silence them and move on. Don't antagonise them. If they're drunk, it can make the situation much worse.

If you have an antagonistic heckler, its best to talk to the audience and not the heckler.

For example, if you wanted to take the sting out of a line, it's best if you don't get personal. You can do this by delivering the line to the audience and not the heckler.

Imagine there's a drunk heckler. You walk over, stand in front of him, and say:

"We could have a battle of wits, but you're unarmed."

It's too direct. If the heckler is already in a bad mood, this approach will make them worse.

The line can be made less threatening by delivering it to the audience in general:

*"We could have a battle of wits, but **he's** unarmed."*

This is much less personal. It should have the effect of defusing the situation and getting the audience on your side.

Remember:

- Only one of you has a mic.
- The audience is on your side (generally, unless BIG JOHN is in).
- You have control of the situation.
- Keep your cool and don't get angry.
- Have good lines in your arsenal to deal with hecklers (both soft and harsher).

General Situations You Can Anticipate and Write For:

One example of this is people talking loudly or whispering during your set. There are a few standard lines used in comedy clubs for this situation. An old faithful is, *"Where did you learn to whisper? A helicopter?"*

Try not to use these standard lines.

There could be a late arrival, a phone going off, people chatting or someone being too drunk.

In Summary

- There are a lot of heckle comeback lines used regularly at comedy clubs all over the world.
- They can be hilarious though generic. Try and write your own. You'll be glad you did.

- Have jokes you can use in typical heckling situations.
- Defuse the heckler and crack on with your set.
- Keep control of the situation with good humor.

It's Your Turn! Take Between Thirty and Sixty Minutes to Complete This Exercise. Good Luck.

Look at these four scenarios:

- Late arrival
- A phone going off
- People chatting
- Someone being drunk

Write as many lines as possible in response to these situations. These comebacks can make or break a gig. Do it well, and you will look like a hero.

Check-in: Do you feel more confident about dealing with hecklers now?

The fear of hecklers doesn't match the reality.

Imagine you were in a pub with a group of mates on a night out. One drunk guy occasionally chips in, talking loudly over your favorite punchlines. Annoying, yes, but the end of the world? No. Keep calm and control the situation with humor.

Comedy Timing

Correct timing is crucial to stand-up. Pauses, rhythm, and tempo contribute highly to the success of comedy material.

The pace of the delivery can have a substantial impact on its comedic effect or even alter its meaning. The same is true for more physical comedy, like slapstick.

Proper timing will showcase your material at its best.

Whether you're pausing to allow for audience laughter or building the suspense to a punchline, it's all about timing.

New comedians often worry about getting the timing right. Still, like delivery skills, chances are you're already using comedy timing when you tell stories to friends. Your comedy timing will get better as you watch successful comedians, practice, and stage your timing.

Pausing for Laughter

You can use silences as set-ups, to let the anticipation build with the audience.

Your audience *cannot laugh and listen to you at the same time*. The minute you start talking, the audience's laughter will shut down.

They'll want to listen to what you're saying, so don't speak during audience laughter. Find the confidence to wait, but not long enough for the room to hit silent.

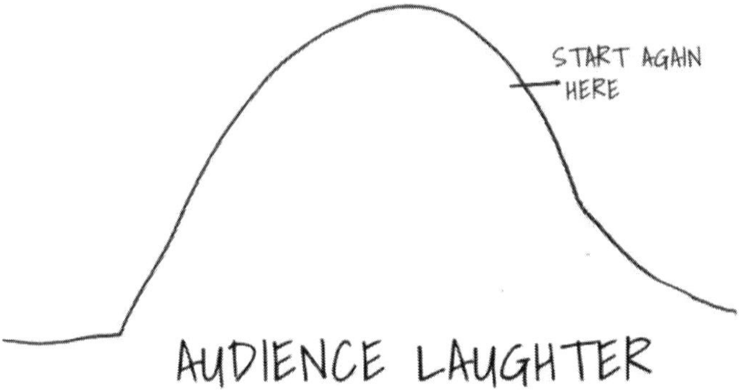

Laughter levels will be relative to the size of the audience. A larger audience will generally need longer to laugh, keeping in mind how contagious laughter can be.

There is also a pregnant pause. A beat which allows an audience to react to a joke or heightens the suspense before the punchline is delivered.

Beats themselves can become a source of humor. Beats such as these give the audience the impression, you're super confident.

If you struggle to pause during your set, write the word "PAUSE" into your material.

Lists

Lists works well in comedy. When a comedian reels off one thing after another to make a point, they finish with the funniest.

I have a graduate who shares her reasons for not having children. It's a long list, which she reels off with perfect rapid-fire timing: *bam, bam, bam.*

You can build momentum with lists. Lists work best when they're reeled off quickly, getting a little louder right up to the end punchline. This often results in cheers from the audience, who are impressed the comedian's remembered everything they just said.

What makes a successful gig - 90% delivery and 10% timing or 90% material and 10% delivery?

There are several schools of thought around this. Material, timing, and delivery are all major contributing factors for a good gig. Don't get too hung up on the stats. Just keep writing and editing your material and strive to improve your performance skills.

It's Your Turn! Take Between Thirty and Sixty Minutes to Complete this Exercise. Good Luck.

Watch footage of the following comedians:

Jerry Seinfeld

Amy Schumer

Jimmy Carr

Eddie Izzard

Richard Pryor

These comedians nail comedy timing. Watch their pauses, tempo, and rhythm. Think about how to apply these to your performance.

Check-in: Do you feel you have a better grasp of comedy timing from watching these comedians?

Did you notice how they pause before punchlines, are silent when they want to build momentum, and then build speed and volume for the crescendo of their gigs?

Have you started integrating timing into your own set? If not, start adding these techniques when practicing your material on and off stage.

Comedy Journey Case Study

Louise works as a Children's Party Entertainer, Ceilidh Caller & DJ. She came into the course to challenge herself. She wanted to see if she could be funny. Louise insists she's not naturally funny, but I disagree.

Louise enjoyed the practical side of the course, standing up, and trying to get laughs.

"The training helped me lots! It gave me the writing techniques to create and refine material. It also helped with the discipline of writing. I learned lots about delivery, timing, and stage craft.

It was loads of fun, and I made some good friends too. I learned ways of writing material which made me enjoy the process. Something I never thought possible.

The comedy coach was loads of fun and super encouraging. She was able to tell when something wasn't funny without discouraging you, offering ways to tweak ideas to get the most out of them."

On graduation night, Louise was excited but nervous. She was concerned about remembering her material and whether it would be well received.

"After the gig, I was on a high. I loved having the other course members to share it with. The learning and rehearsing experience from the course made the first gig really smooth, and it felt natural."

I asked Louise if she had noticed a shift in her confidence levels due to the course?

"Even though I'm used to performing regularly, my confidence has definitely increased. I'm able to perform in a different way and trust myself to write. I did my stand-up gig as a ventriloquist and the puppet got a much better reaction from an adult audience than I would have ever imagined."

Louise is amazed at how many genuinely funny people there are on the comedy circuit.

"As someone who doesn't think they're naturally funny, I've been surprised that being funny can actually be learnt. I worried it might be competitive, but folks are friendly, helpful and encouraging."

I asked Louise what she found challenging about stand-up.
"I was taken aback at just how long it takes to write a decent five-minute set. And stand-up in pubs isn't like stand up you see on TV. Everyone isn't always sitting there quietly listening intently to what you say. You've got to win them over and deal with the general noise and chatter in the room. This can be distracting so you need to know your material well."

Louise is in the throes of a house move but can't wait to do stand-up again. Another one bites the dust!

How to Get a Gig

Check Point

Are you keen to start gigging?

How's your writing developing?

Are you ready for your first gig?

Are you prepared?

Your Comedy Set

When you think you have your first comedy set prepared, here are a few questions worth asking:

- Do you find your set funny?
- Would you be proud to show it to your best mate?
- Are you keen to say it?
- Does it stretch you as a performer?
- Is it the best of you?

Make sure you know your set well enough to build a rapport with your audience. Knowing your material allows your confidence to shine.

How to Book Your First Gig

Years ago, I would just show up for open mic nights, speak to the person running the gig, and bag a spot.

Some open mic nights will still allow you to do this. However, many promoters will ask for short biographies, online biographies, and quotes before they will allow you to perform.

Footage from a past performance is also a standard ask.

If you're lucky enough to get into a Brighton Comedy Course, you'll be in possession of a professional film reel of your graduation gig in front of a large, live audience.

The film is ideal for promoters, as it will probably be the biggest gig you'll do in the early stages of your stand-up career. Plus, promoters will be impressed by the standard.

If you'd like to see some of the first-ever graduation gigs, go to YouTube and search "Brighton Comedy Course." You can subscribe for comedy tips and new graduation performances.

With the popularity of technology, including mobile phones, it's become much more common for a comedian to be asked to provide a performance clip. For this reason, it's good to get into the habit of recording your gigs.

Recording your gigs works on a few different levels:

1. You may end up capturing footage of when you're on a roll and the audience is laughing loudly.
2. You can look back at the footage afterwards and find out what worked well and what needs improvement.

Ask someone to record your gig for you (but not the compere, as they have a lot on).

Promoters may ask for a short biography instead of a showreel. How creative you are with this is up to you. However, if you're still on open mic nights, don't say you're the closing act for *The Comedy Store*. If you're lying, it's likely you'll be found out.

If you've gigged at decent clubs, list them! Ditto if you've worked alongside high-profile comedians.

The comedy community is a close-knit place, so promoters may ask the comedians you mention what they thought of your act. So, keep it as real as possible.

Your biography should include:

- Name and contact details
- A summary of you and your set
- Any competition success
- Clubs worked
- Comedians worked with
- Links to any footage
- Quotes from reviews or other, more famous, acts

There are several websites where you can find example biographies. You can also add one of your own.

There's The Cheeky Monkey's site in Birmingham https://www.comedycv.co.uk/.

There is also an open comedy site which lists comedians from all over the world.
https://www.opencomedy.com/UK/comedians.

Twenty years ago, I'd go to a comedy night and speak to the promoter directly. I think this is the best way to do it.

Speaking to the promoter is easier at smaller gigs. Email was a common way to book a gig. These days, I've found Facebook to be the most popular platform on which promoters book gigs.

Most big cities have an abundance of comedy nights. Check your local *What's On* guide or do a simple Google search for a list of your nearest open mic nights.

It's unlikely you'll book an open spot in a bigger club initially, but it's always worth a try. A few of the bigger clubs have Gong or New Act nights, which are excellent ways to get your foot in the door. Just make sure you're ready to shine.

Go to local gigs at every opportunity.

A Google search might not provide the promoter's name, but this information is easy to find out from the bar staff or the comedians.

At the beginning of a comedy night, the promoter is generally busy sorting the room layout, saying hello to the audience, and giving the running order to the comedians.

If you are prepared and hoping to pick up a gig that night, wait until the promoter is free and confidently introduce yourself to him or her. Keep your introduction short and sweet.

"Hi, my name is … I'm working on the comedy circuit doing open spots. I'd love a spot tonight if there are any no-shows.

If not, it would be great to book for another night. How should I get in touch? Facebook? Email?"

If you're not hoping to do a gig that night, then wait until the interval or the end of the show. You might have a better chance of gaining their attention.

You'll have a bigger chance of bagging the gig if you're confident.

I wouldn't mention it's your first gig. Some promoters will be cool with it, but I don't think pointing it out is necessary.

Whether or not you perform that night, take in the room for future reference. Is there any comedy in it? Is there scary art on the walls or sofas that you can't get out of?

During the interval or at the end of the show, say hello to the comedians who performed. If you liked their sets, **tell them so.** Mention you're working the circuit and hoping to pick up a few gigs. Ask for recommendations. Some may have a list of promoters in the area and will offer to send you their information. Networking within the comedy community is the best way to pick up gigs.

It's Your Turn! Spend Two Hours Completing this Exercise. Good Luck.

1. Read over the notes you took from this book. Digest what you've learned so far.

2. Perform your material while recording it and watch it back.

Ready to Book Your First Gig?

Answer these questions as fully as you can.

- Are you ready for your first gig?
- Off the top of your head, write down everything you've learned about stand up so far.
- How much material have you written?
- Do you have material you're excited to use?
- Have you got a punchy five-minute set you can perform without notes?
- Have you integrated what you've learnt about delivery, timing, and performance to bring about the best gig you can?
- Have you absorbed the performance tips to bring about a confident performance?

Check-in: Only you know if you're ready. Remember, being nervous is natural. You'll need nervous excitement to have a good gig. By this point, you've learned lots about comedy, written plenty of material, watched great comedians in action, and observed the learning points by completing the exercises.

Are you confident in your material and feel you're ready to give it your all?

Then, Let's Get Your First Gig Booked!

Follow the steps from the last chapter and get the date in the diary. Your first gig will likely take place a bit in the future, so you'll have time to do any last-minute polishing of your act. Keep rehearsing your gig and have faith in what you have. On gig night, remember to breathe and enjoy. Comedy is supposed to be fun!

GOOD LUCK - KICK ARSE!

If you're not feeling quite there yet, re-read the chapters with which you believe you need the most help. Then write more and perform at home. Pencil in a date to repeat this chapter when you're feeling ready to do your first gig.

Congratulations

You did it! You performed your first comedy gig!

How was it? Did you take time to write down what worked and what didn't for both your material and your performance? If not, do it now.

What was challenging? Could you anticipate solutions to challenges for future gigs?

How was your confidence level? Did you harness your nervous excitement?

Did you remember everything you learnt?

The Buzz after - Did you get it? There's nothing in the world like it.

I didn't get the buzz on my first gig, but I got it pretty regularly after, and it's just such a joy!

Don't worry if you didn't precisely smash it. You'll get there with hard work and determination.

It's a real achievement to do a stand-up gig and, if you have, then the experience will always be yours. Performing a stand-up gig is a game-changer!

Continue to use your journal. Continue writing comedy and monitoring your progress.

YOU SHOULD BE ESPECIALLY PROUD OF YOURSELF. WELL DONE!

What Next?

Here we are at the end of *How to be a Comedian and Smash your first Gig.*

This book aimed to cover the most important aspects of being a Stand-up Comedian and get you to perform your first gig.

When it comes to comedy, theory alone is not enough. That's the reason why the writing and performance exercises have played such a significant role in this book. I hope you got lots out of the book and it has given you the motivation and know-how to go on and do the job.

If you're wondering what to do next, check out *The New Comedians Handbook* which has more in-depth information on the next stage of your journey.

The book will provide writing exercises to help you produce a whole new set of comedy material. It will cover everything you need to continue building your knowledge and momentum and to help you enhance your skills. It will also give you insights on how to progress in the comedy industry.

The New Comedians Handbook Contains:

- Starting on the Comedy Circuit
- Comedians Etiquette
- Action Plans for Success
- Comedy Competitions
- Compering
- Women in Comedy
- Getting sick of your material?
- Running your own Comedy Night
- Being an organised Comedian

- Dealing with a Tough gig
- Finding your Voice
- Comedy Facebook Groups and Forums
- How to find an Agent
- How to Progress in the Comedy Industry
- Summary and Comedy Circuit tips

You can also:

- Book 1-2-1 Comedy Coaching with me, either in person or through virtual coaching.
- Have a Performance Critique: Send up to ten minutes of your material for individual feedback.
- Come to the full Beginners comedy course.
- Book one of our Comedy Holiday Weekenders which happen all over. Get in touch if you'd like to suggest one in your area.
- Book me to speak at your events.
- Buy Gift vouchers for £20, £50 or £100
- Take one of our online Comedy or Creative Writing Courses on the Thinkific platform.

Check out www.brightoncomedycourse.com for these services.

It has been a pleasure working with you.

May your comedy journey be long and fruitful!

Keep sharing your funny.

What Did You Think of ***How to be a Comedian and Smash your first Gig?***

First of all, thank you for purchasing this book. I know you could have picked any number of books to read, but you picked this book and for that I am extremely grateful.

I hope that this book has added more confidence, knowledge, and humour to your everyday life, as well as your comedy life. If so, and you have found some benefit in reading this, please you could take some time to post a review on Amazon or Good Reads.

Your feedback and support will help me greatly.

And if you could share this book with your friends and family by posting to **Facebook** , **Instagram** and **Twitter**, that would be very much appreciated. Who knows, they may become funnier as a result and join you on the comedy circuit!

Thanks again. Good Luck.